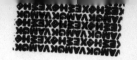

P9-CQO-435

FURNITURE DECORATION
MADE EASY

FURNITURE DECORATION
MADE EASY

A practical work manual for decorating furniture by stenciling,
gold-leaf application and freehand painting

BY

CHARLES HALLETT

DRAWINGS BY THE AUTHOR

CHARLES T. BRANFORD CO., *Publishers*
BOSTON, MASSACHUSETTS

Library of Congress catalog card number: 52-10670

Printed in the United States of America
The Murray Printing Company, Massachusetts

ACKNOWLEDGEMENT

It would have been impossible to assemble the old patterns in this book except for the fine cooperation and long-time patronage through the years of the following individuals and antique dealers. To these for their continued help and encouragement the author is certainly grateful.

Benjamin Altman Co., New York, N. Y.

Aunt Lydia's Attic, Waban, Mass.

Mr. and Mrs. Harry Ball, Brookfield, Mass.

Mrs. Bruce Barton, New York, N. Y.

Mrs. Anna Benjamin, Portland, Maine

Mr. Paul Blanchard, Moultonboro, N. H.

Mrs. David Bramman, Medfield, Mass.

Mrs. Maud Brown, Boston, Mass.

Mr. Ralph W. Burnham, Ipswich, Mass.

Walter D. Carr, Wellesley, Mass.

Mr. Charles Carruth, Rochester, N. Y.

Mrs. Edwin F. Cary, Providence, R. I.

Cooley's China Shop, Boston, Mass.

Mrs. William A. Copeland, Mansfield, Mass.

Mr. Michael Coscia, Boston, Mass.

Miss Josephine Farrin, Amherst, N. H.

Federal Willow Co., Boston, Mass.

Richard R. Fine and Sons, Boston, Mass.

Mr. Fred Finnerty, Boston, Mass.

Mr. Harold P. Fuller, Newton, Mass.

Paul and Amy Gott, Lowell, Mass.

Mrs. Leaman F. Hallett, Mansfield, Mass.

Mr. Robert M. Higgins, Hancock, N. H.

Mr. Charles King, West Barnstable, Mass.

Mrs. Jane Lasalle, Marblehead, Mass.

Mrs. James F. Leitch, Philadelphia, Pa.

R. H. Macy Co., New York, N. Y.

Mr. Stacy Marble, Marblehead, Mass.

Marshall Field Co., Chicago, Ill.

Mrs. Harry Merchant, Reading, Mass.

Miracle Americana, New York, N. Y.

Mount Auburn Antique Shop, Cambridge, Mass.

Old Furniture Shop, Provincetown, Mass.

Mr. T. W. Rhodes, Lynn, Mass.

Mr. Maurice Shapiro, Boston, Mass.

Mrs. May Simmons, Peacedale, R. I.

Mr. Everett Spaulding, Georgetown, Mass.

Mr. Maurice Spaulding, Georgetown, Mass.

The Stewarts, Needham, Mass.

Mr. Frank F. Sylvia, Nantucket, Mass.

Mr. Louis Tallier, formerly with George Lord

John Wanamaker, New York, N. Y.

Mr. Hyman G. Webber, Hampton, N. H.

Mr. Max Webber, Middleton, Mass.

Mr. A. A. Yeaton, Hillsboro, N. H.

FOREWORD

*How happy is he born or taught
That serveth not another's will;
Whose armour is his honest thought,
And simple truth his utmost skill!*

SIR HENRY WOTTEN

It is a long time since that spring of 1919 when Alice Van Leer Carrick's delightful book, "Collector's Luck," appeared. In Chapter II on stenciled furniture she seems for the first time in this century to bring general attention to the charm and enduring qualities of stenciling on trays, Hitchcock chairs and Boston rockers.

The Model T Ford has given way to the Futuramic and the V/8 engine. Likewise, in our striving for the new in the home, the antique piece and its copies has often given way to Swedish Modern and over-simplified "blond" utilitarian furniture. Nevertheless, there is today probably more interest in acquiring those charming old stenciled pieces and their decorated reproductions than at any time since their universal popularity in the nineteenth century.

Little did Alice Van Leer Carrick dream of what a tidal wave of furniture would be stenciled later, when she wrote in 1919: "Nobody works with the stencil now — the 'feeling' and the 'soul' has vanished; still I think it is a craft that could as well be revived as weaving of blankets." She could hardly foresee the thousands of home craftsmen, or rather craftswomen, who since have tried their hand at it; craftswomen so artistically successful in stenciling their own handiwork to cherish and hand down.

The purpose of this book is to: (1) help the amateur attain a better understanding of the old methods of furniture decorating; (2) show many patterns collected by author since 1924 from thousands of old chairs, bureaus and tables which he has restored; (3) show the different types of chairs made so extensively throughout the eastern part of the country and primarily to show which type of decoration best fitted this furniture; (4) if, as in most cases, the antique is not readily available, to show the *reproduction* and its fitness for decorating with the old patterns.

This handbook on furniture decoration is not intended as an exhaustive reference work on the history of stenciling, nor on the lives of the early artisans. The principal benefits you may obtain by a careful study of its contents are: (1) explicit instructions for the amateur, (2) short cuts we have learned by many years of decorating, (3) ideas for applying the old patterns to the vast amount of reproduction furniture easily obtainable today.

If we can make one enthusiast more nearly approach the perfection of the better originals we will consider that this book has served its ultimate purpose.

In studying and analyzing the early craftsmen's work on individual chairs, we feel that their interpretation of design had that spark of genius behind it that elevated it to true art. W. C. Brownell in his profound book, "The Genius of Style," finds the spirit that motivated these early artisans. "In the widest sense, thus, style would be the art of technic, that element of technical expression which makes an art of what otherwise is at best but skill. . . . The genius of style operates through a fusion of order and movement. . . . Doubtless order is nature's and art's as well as Heaven's first law." These early craftsmen had primarily enormous energy, and as Matthew Arnold says, "Genius is mainly an affair of energy — the infiltration of a worker's conscious art by his personal whim." How well that definition fits is aptly illustrated by the photographs and patterns of old decorations pictured in this book.

CONTENTS

HAND-PAINTED BUREAU, ABOUT 1840

CHAPTER I

Work does more than get us our living;
It gets us our life.

HENRY FORD

BACKGROUND OF FURNITURE DECORATION

Evolution of American Furniture Styles

The gradual evolution of styles in furniture design during the eighteenth and early nineteenth centuries was an exact index of the increasing prosperity of the early colonies and the new Federal state. It would almost seem that the increasing skill of the widely scattered local cabinetmakers had a direct relation to this increased flow of wealth.

Cabinetmakers were the forerunners of furniture factories. Prior to the Revolution, furniture in this country was strictly an individual expression of the workman's skill. No factories had been established. Each cabinetmaker had his individual style. The wainscot and three-slat Pilgrim chairs 1640–1700, the lighter four-slat ladderback 1680–1760, the bannisterback 1700–1770, the seven and nine spindle hoop and fanback Windsor 1715–1765, were made of local woods. The easiest obtainable were maple, pine, oak, ash and birch. Naturally there was considerable English influence in design, but as the American cabinetmakers developed they leaned less and less on old country influence. The best workmen here evolved an individual utilitarian technique that placed them in the forefront.

Increased commerce and prosperity had a vast influence on furniture styles. When our sailing ships traveled the seven seas they brought back new ideas and new expensive furniture to grace the early mansions of the wealthier merchants. Pine and maple gradually gave place to mahogany and walnut, plain and burled and crotch-figured veneer. With this new mahogany and increased skill American cabinetmakers reached their apex. Men like John Goddard of Rhode Island, William Savery of Philadelphia, and later Duncan Phyfe of New York, of course, were directly inspired by

Thomas Chippendale, Thomas Sheraton, and George Hepplewhite, all of England; yet the American cabinetmakers refined and simplified the English designs so skillfully that their pieces today in the museums seem to exceed in charm those of their English masters.

Furniture Painted

It is important to know how and why *painted furniture* became so universally popular and easily purchased by the not-so-wealthy early Americans. The first painted chairs to make their appearance in the colonies were American Windsor, bannister-back and arrowback chairs as well as the very necessary chests. At an early period they were painted black, or Indian dull red, which often was made of a mixture of red powder and milk, gray in a soft, dull shade, and sometimes a dark green known then as "coachpainter's green." After the light but sturdy rush bottom chairs were originated by George Hepplewhite and Thomas Sheraton in England, the vogue for painted furniture, with slightly less ornate decoration than used in England, rapidly spread over America. American Sheraton chairs were made from 1785 to about 1820.

Old Masters

Influence of George Hepplewhite and Thomas Sheraton; the Adam Brothers; the artist, Angelica Kauffman. The Hepplewhite style, 1785–1810, was earlier than Sheraton, 1790–1820. The chairs were painted an oyster white, a pinkish ivory, soft yellow obtained from England in powder form, now known as "India Rubber yellow," which was really arsenic-pentasulphide, light green obtained by mixing this yellow with Prussian blue, and sometimes a soft red, which resembles a lively, deeper terra-cotta. Most of the Hepplewhite influence chairs had square rush seats with very thin finishing bands or no bands at all.

1

An American adaptation of the upholstered square-seated, often shieldback English Adam Brothers and Hepplewhite chairs was quite varied. The Sheraton rush seated chair became known as Sheraton Fancy chair. Considerable heavier than those of Hepplewhite influence, the rush seat had usually a rounded front known as "guitar-bottom." The American cabinetmakers certainly used their imaginations on these Sheraton Fancy chairs. We have personally seen about a hundred different variants: wide and narrow top back panels, horizontal and perpendicular secondary back panels and stretchers, always simple turned legs with gilt turnings, and usually decorated front legs. Bamboo turned Sheratons with gilt balls, usually painted pale yellow with orange and black brush-work decoration, were of Chinese influence. The arms might be delicately turned, but more often were of bent oak or of ash in hoop form. Some idea of the variety is gained by illustrations, page 107.

The front stretcher on these Sheratons was almost always adapted to gold-leaf decoration. See Chapter IX, page 107, for instructions in decorating Sheraton Fancy chairs with patterns.

French Empire Influence

The transition and Empire or Greek Revival Period, 1815–1830; the Regency Period influence merging into the Hitchcock and Hitchcock type chair, 1826–1850. About 1815, influenced by the French Empire period and English Regency classicism, American cabinetmakers adapted the curves and ornate French designs to simpler American living. In place of the applied brass mounts and ormolu elaborations, gold leaf and stenciling were introduced at considerable less cost. The effect was not only pleasing, but far more in keeping with American simplicity.

Here in New York the embellishment of fine mahogany furniture with gold leaf and metallic gold powders was undoubtedly the earliest stenciling done on furniture in this country. The acanthus leaf variations and repeat unit borders, with fruit often combined with flowers, made the Empire pieces distinctive.

Striping on Furniture

Wide and narrow gold-leaf stripes *took the place* of expensive satinwood inlay strips so common on Hepplewhite pieces. English Sheraton pieces had thin brass lines inserted in the rosewood or mahog-

any veneers. The Hepplewhite had inlaid satinwood strips. It seems incredible that this vogue for neoclassic adaptation should gain such universal favor in England during the reign of George IV, which ended in 1830, and that of William IV, which ended in 1837. Yet such was the case, and moreover it "took hold" here in America with almost as much popular form. The adaptation of the Regency here was of course the parent and immediate cause of the decorated Fancy chair and the Hitchcock and its adaptations.

Periods of Chair Makers

The earliest decorated chairs were the Sheratons or those that show more Hepplewhite influence. They were mostly decorated in gold or metal leaf — a leaf thicker than gold leaf called Dutch metal leaf (an alloy of copper and zinc) and considerably cheaper than gold leaf. Silver leaf was also used, and under many coats of orange shellac it gave the final effect of gold.

An outline index of the sequence of chair manufacture in this country is:

American Sheraton, 1785–c. 1820
American Empire, which includes the so-called Baltimore Hitchcock, 1814–c. 1835
Lambert Hitchcock, 1826–1829
Hitchcock and Alford, 1829–1843
Union Chair Company, 1843–1850

American Chair Labels

Signatures on various forms of Hitchcock and other types have been found stenciled on the back of the seat as follows:

Hitchcock, Hitchcockville, Conn. Warranted.
Hitchcock and Alford Co., Hitchcockville, Conn. Warranted.
Union Chair Co., West Winsted, Conn.
D. Churchill & Co., Curtisville, M.
William Moore, Jr.
Holmes and Roberts, Colebrook, Conn. Warranted.
Only a very few stenciled chairs have been signed by W. P. Eaton; (see article in *Antiques Magazine*, August 1949, by Olive C. Robinson).

The American Sheraton chair was made principally in New York, although L. Hitchcock is credited with making at least the knocked-down parts to be locally assembled.

CHAPTER II

Real joy comes not from ease or riches or from praise of men,
But from doing something worth while.

SIR WILFRED GRENFELL

EARLY CRAFTSMEN —
HOW TO EMULATE THEM

Brilliance of Early Stenciling

Early stenciling was executed meticulously with real gold powder, then obtainable at sixteen dollars an ounce — and an ounce went a long way. This use of real gold powder accounts for the almost miraculous brilliance these early pieces have after nearly one hundred and fifty years. Moreover, the varnish used was a superior coach varnish made by secret processes and unobtainable today.

Example of Early Craftsmanship

Most craftsmen who read this book are familiar with the work on the early Hitchcock chairs. But if interested in the real acme of stenciling, it would be worth their while to visit the American Wing of the Metropolitan Museum of Art in New York. An excellent example is the piano in mahogany by John Tallman dated about 1835. It might very well have been stenciled by Thomas Gildersleeve, the American pioneer in stencil art.

Need for Inspiration Today

The stenciled piece is an inspiration. The workmanship shows the values of light and shade gradations — the texture of stenciling as a fine art in itself. The stenciling contrasts vividly in depth with the more definite, harder gold leaf, which was etched. An amateur looking at this masterpiece will certainly strive harder for perfection, and realize that the hasty methods used in the later mass production period are no criterion to follow in his own work.

Strive for the Best Grade of Work

It has been our idea all these years of commercial stenciling to copy and follow only the best and early patterns and methods. We can say at the outset, if you do not "Hitch your wagon to a star" you will not go too far in the ancient art of stenciling. It always pays to pick the best patterns, which might or might not be the most intricate. They can be used over and over again, and if executed properly, the work will have a high standard. On the other hand, if you use a rather cheap one-piece design, so often seen and copied, it will inevitably lower your standard. Contrary to some of the books on the subject, stenciling is not primarily an easy way to have fun. It is rather a serious business, or a creative hobby.

Progress in Perfection

Constantly strive to approach the early masterpieces. Try to make each piece you work on a little better than the piece done before. The early workmen spent long tedious years of apprenticeship before they arrived at such perfection. By no means is this meant for discouragement, but rather it is intended as a guide for your interest in this most satisfying of the truly American arts. If this idea of betterment is kept in mind you will be amazed at the progress made. You will look at last year's work, and at the year's before that, and realize how far you have progressed. Quite possibly you will wish to do some of your pieces over. If so, you are decidedly on the right road to perfection.

Pieces often Decorated

In addition to the thousands of chairs turned out from 1828 to after the Civil War, and stenciled in widely separated factories, many other pieces of furniture have the same patterns identical or in variation: beds, bureaus, two-level washstands, stools, settees, cradles or rockers, bellows, boxes large and small, all found a ready market in the public eager to buy anything that was decorated.

3

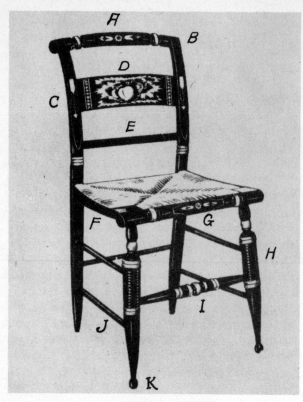

ANATOMY OF CHAIR

A Turned bolster top
B Top of stile, usually decorated on *any* antique chair
C Back post on stile
D Back splat or panel. Main decoration
E Secondary back panel or splat
F Seat (when rush, finished on sides with cut-out thin wooden strips)
G Turned front roll or seat front turning, usually decorated
H Turned leg (turnings called rings)
I Front stretcher or rungs (turned)
J Side stretcher or rungs
K Ball or button foot

TWO TYPES OF STENCILING

A. THE *FLAT* NO SHADE ONE-PIECE STENCIL

This depended on its outline or silhouette for interest. It was applied principally on front seat rolls of Hitchcock chairs and on the side posts or stiles; on top panel corners of Boston rockers and on the front seat roll; on rockers with arms and the armless sewing or "nursing rocker." It was used not so often on Sheraton chairs, which usually had etched gold leaf. It was widely used in conventional borders on dressing tables around the top edges and anywhere the intricate cutting in solid gold powder would embellish the effect. These borders were often used on the better-executed Boston rockers along the back of the seat. Only in the later mass production or decline of the art

were these one-piece stencils with no shadings used as a central motif on a chair splat.

William Page Eaton

The one exception to this general observation was the intricate and interesting "occupational" stencils cut by the great master of the art, William Page Eaton, born in Salem, Massachusetts on April 2, 1819, died near New Boston, New Hampshire, in 1904. His animals, men in boats, horses and carriages, and interesting local activities were cut with great precision of action and natural motion.

These one-piece silhouettes in gold powder placed as a central motif on any piece would readily draw attention. They added greatly to the popularity of all stenciled furniture of that period. Eaton's fiddleback or bannister single piece stencils were *masterpieces of intricate cutting.* Eaton had as many as twenty odd patterns for the back splat of a "fiddle." Strange to say, only a very few of these have ever turned up today. We have seen only three that we could identify.

B. THE SHADED METHOD OF FRUIT AND FLOWER GROUPINGS WITH LEAVES; ALSO, LESS OFTEN SEEN SHELL GROUPINGS

The pineapple (symbol of hospitality) was often used as a central unit; see illustration on page 32. It was composed of two or more parts: the base, the fruit section and the top spines. Around this were often massed pears, peaches, plums (these in one or two parts), cherries, pomegranates, berries, grapes in bunches and individually shaded, currants and the often seen lime and melon in varying sizes. The strawberry seems to be ever present.

Built-Up or Superimposed Stencils

The strawberry is a good example of the superimposed stencil. The fruit part was in red or copper bronze upon which was then stenciled the seed and the hull in separate units, usually in contrasting silver powder. The strawberry was often used each side of a heavy group of fruit to finish out the "rhythm" of the design. It seemed to be the practice in all the best stenciling to "feather out" the heavier fruit with these smaller units and the strawberry was one used frequently. This "feathering out" process is illustrated by drawings on page 32 and the "feathering out" units are illustrated on page 38.

Where this massed fruit motif was used, much greater skill was needed than where the fruit units are placed in a central basket or dish.

4

Multi-Unit or Compound Grouping

We believe the most interesting groupings of all were the massed fruit and flower combinations. See illustration on page 33. These were often composed of peaches, limes, pears, and two-part roses, with intricate wheat sheaves and leaves with shaded veins fading the interest away with some interesting tiny "feathering out" unit interspersed with the leaves. Right here, if you hit on some fine combination of fruit and flower grouping as you progress with your stenciling, by all means preserve it at once. You may not remember it exactly next week. Stencil it on a piece of cardboard that has been painted with flat black paint. You may not have the proper inspiration when you want it again, and by recording it on cardboard you have the grouping "nailed" down permanently for future use and reference.

Early Craftsmen Were Masters of Grouping

We will make the statement from the very outset that what made the early stencilers like Gildersleeve, Eaton, Jarred Johnson and George Lord such master craftsmen was their uncanny ability *to group the hundreds of units in their folios artistically and to fit them to the space unit.* Always assembled with such studied nicety! They had a sense of the utter fitness and logic on the use of the units in filling space on each type of chair. When found to be exactly right, a pattern was used over and over on that type of chair as a sort of standard decoration. Of course, the precision of cutting a stencil was all-important, even to the most minute curvature of a leaf or tendril. Instruction in cutting the stencil is taken up at length in Chapter IV. After examining hundreds of original designs over a period of years, we are ever impressed by the closeness of these motifs to the natural leaves and flowers of the gardens and fields of New England.

Style in Decoration Was Related to the Old Way of Life

Speaking of those early craftsmen and the particular and understanding clientele they served and strove to please, it is altogether fitting that the readers of this technical book do some research themselves on this golden era of American living. How can one separate the vivid personalities of the genteel colonists and the early Federalists from their classical houses and the furniture that surrounded their daily living over the years?

W. C. Brownell says, "To secure permanence in the aesthetic product the preservative quality of the latter element (style) is needed. Without it, art is as fleeting as fashion. None the less, it cannot be gainsaid that personality is the most interesting thing in the world. Therefore, expressing itself in style, achieves at once the most interesting and the most lasting aesthetic result."

This deep understanding of the motivating force behind a craftsman or artist by W. C. Brownell, long forgotten critic of art and literature, creates for us a link between the early decorators and their patrons and the collectors today of their handiwork. Their work today has survived because the mind they put into it was deeper than the fleeting fashion of the period.

Biographical Notes

Thomas Chippendale, born (unknown), died 1779. Author of the monumental work, "The Gentleman and Cabinet Maker's Director" 1754, which contained engraved plates, 2d Edition 1759, 3d Edition 1762. George Hepplewhite, born (unknown), died 1786. Author of "The Cabinetmaker and Upholsterer's Guide," 1788.

Hepplewhite's furniture legs were slender, plain, fluted or reeded, tapering to a spade foot. He originated the wing chair, also the painted chair. The Hepplewhite style succumbed in his day, and even down to today's reproductions, to the eternal enemy of all art, the uninspired banality of the average man.

Angelica Kauffmann 1741–1807, born in Coire, Switzerland, daughter of a poor, mediocre painter whose fame was only his success in teaching his precocious daughter. At twelve years of age she was a portrait painter. In 1754 her father took her to Milan, Italy. She spoke Italian, German, French and English. In 1766 she came to England with Lady Wentworth, wife of the Italian ambassador to London. She first painted a portrait of Garrick and became a warm friend of Sir Joshua Reynolds, and was one of the founders of the Royal Academy in 1769, date of their first catalogue. From 1769 to 1782 she painted trays, decorated furniture made by Hepplewhite, painted and exhibited portraits each year at the Academy. Thus she was probably the *original* tray and furniture decorator. In 1781 she married the Venetian artist, Antonio Zucchi, and went to Rome forthwith, where she lived for twenty-five years, regaining her old painting and social prestige.

Lambert Hitchcock, born in Cheshire, Connecticut June 28, 1795. So many adequate and detailed notes and biographies have been written about this remarkable man that we will confine these notes to the barest outline.

In 1818, at the age of twenty-three, he moved to Barkhamsted, Connecticut, where his first factory was established near the bountiful wood supplies, and where he could utilize the water power of the Farmington River. Here he made chair parts, which were shipped mostly south and west to be assembled near the chair trade.

Lambert Hitchcock, one of the shrewdest of Connecticut Yankees, despite his continuous financial difficulties, invented the Hitchcock chair and innovated its outstanding features. He knew, for instance, that for strength the back legs of a chair should go entirely to the top connecting turning. He knew that the rush seat was much more comfortable than the wooden or plank seat. He realized that a decorated chair was a much more salable article than previous plain chairs. Moreover, he could vary the back splat or splats in many forms to add to the selling appeal. In 1826 his selling genius had such success that he built his factory at Hitchcockville, Connecticut.

While it is generally believed that the Boston and Salem rocker was invented in or around Boston, Hitchcock was the first to make them in quantity in Connecticut. He certainly originated the Cape Cod rocker or rockee, with demountable baby-retaining rack. These were sold extensively at forty cents a foot. A five footer brought two dollars, while the common Boston rocker then brought a dollar and a half each. His misfortune was in customers not paying cash and in stiff competition. In 1829 he failed, but after three years he paid all debts, and in 1832 went into partnership with Arba Alford, Jr., his capable superintendent, whose sister he married in 1830.

It seems to be an accepted fallacy that all turtleback "Hitchcocks" came from Connecticut. They were also produced in great numbers in Ashburnham, Massachusetts, around 1830. See illustration on page 73 of an authentic Ashburnham turtleback.

In 1842 the Hitchcock and Alford partnership was dissolved, and Lambert moved to Unionville, where in business alone he labeled his chairs "Lambert Hitchcock, Unionville, Connecticut." Arba and his brother, Alfred Alford, continued the old business at Hitchcockville until 1862.

STENCILED OR GOLD-LEAF BORDERS FOR TABLES, BUREAU TOPS, ETC.
Actual Size

It is revealing how much work can be accomplished with a minimum list of necessities; however, as you progress and expand your hobby, many more items will, of necessity, become indispensable. Paints and materials starred are absolutely essential. Other items can be purchased as work progresses.

BRUSHES

For Removing Paint: almost any old two-inch width brush; a common, inexpensive bristle brush, if you purchase one.

For Background Painting: red and other colors, get a good ox-hair or fitch brush chiseled with bristles imbedded in a square soldered tin. For a varnish or shellac brush the shorter haired fitch or ox-hair chiseled is ideal; properly kept, it will last for years.

For Fine Brush Work and Colored Details: at least two red sable square-tipped showcard brushes No. 2 and No. 6. These will last for years, but always buy the *best*. A red sable "twirler" is a great help, but may be hard to obtain.

For Transparent Wide Striping on Chair Backs: Nos. 0, 1, and 2 short-haired squirrel quills, square-tipped on a stick.

For Fine Striping: almost any size very long-haired squirrel striper or dagger striper will do. From this brush, as illustrated on page 8, cut out the necessary number of hairs to make the width stripe you desire.

For very fine details, especially on tin work: small camel's-hair water-color brushes are used professionally (tipped).

Care of Brushes

If you purchase good fitch or ox-hair brushes, which is the best long-run economy, as well as the more fragile squirrel stripers, and especially the sable flat end fine work brushes, they will last indefinitely *only* if given the proper care.

Never let any brush dry hard with paint on the hairs.

After using the fitch or ox-hair brush, suspend it in turpentine; or a shellac brush in denatured alcohol, with the tip not resting on the bottom. An empty large size mayonnaise jar with a hole cut in its metal top to fit the handle is a good container. Bore a small hole through the handle and insert a nail to hold up the brush. The nail rests on top of the jar cover. Another method used is a piece of old inner tube tied over the top with the brush handle inserted in a slit in the rubber.

If your brush is to be put away for some time, clean thoroughly with turpentine, wash with yellow soap and warm water, and wrap up in a piece of waxed paper. It should lie flat. Do not wash sable or squirrel hair brushes with soap and water. Clean them thoroughly with turpentine, wipe dry and draw them between the thumb and forefinger which have been dipped in paraffine oil. Put away on a flat cardboard through which you have sewn pieces of elastic to keep them separated.

PAINTS AND OTHER MATERIALS

(Starred items are required for your decorating.)

The following colors come ground in japan:

Venetian Red: ½ *pint cans and 1 quart cans.* Used extensively thinned with turpentine, it must be long and thoroughly mixed.

Tuscon Red: ½ pint cans. A darker red, almost maroon, used where a very dark red grain is desired for an undercoat. May be mixed with Venetian Red to tone down Venetian, which in itself is a fairly bright yellow-red.

Burnt Sienna comes in ½ pint cans and quarts. Probably the ideal background color for black graining, thinned with gum turpentine.

Permanent Vermilion: ½ pint cans and quarts. A beautiful clear red (not on the yellowish tone) used extensively for carriage and coach painting for countless years. Under an antique glaze varnish, this color assumes a richness unequaled by anything else. Hard to find; made by Willey's who have now given it over to another concern, H. Behlen & Bros.

Tropical Vermilion: half pint cans, slightly brighter than Chinese Vermilion but can be made more orange by adding yellow.

Chrome Yellow Medium: half pint cans, also tubes, used with flat white to make various shades of yellow and used in mixing the antique yellow.

Raw Sienna: half pint cans and tubes. Used in toning down and antiquing.

Raw Umber: half pint cans and tubes. A dark brown opaque color for toning down.

Chrome Green Light: half pint cans, a beautiful green, darker than the name implies and the age-old coachpainter's green. Used under colored varnishes, it is darkened and enriched.

Chrome Green Dark: half pint cans, a very dark green, too dark to be toned down or mixed with burnt umber or other toners.

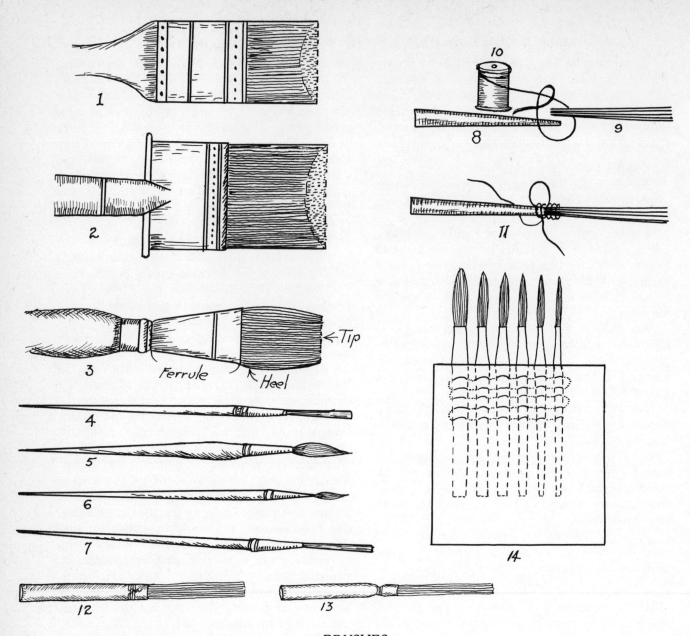

BRUSHES

1. Chiseled varnish or shellac brush, ox-hair or fitch
2. Chiseled paint or shellac brush, soldered tin, ox-hair or fitch
3. Not chiseled camel's-hair or ox-tail varnish brush, comes in various sizes
4. Flat-end red sable utility brush
5. Pointed red sable brush for oil color and fine work
6. Pointed camel's-hair brush for finest black and colored lines
7. Square end red sable "twirler" for scrolls, etc.
8. Cut-off penholder for handle of hairline striper
9. Hairs cut from long quill or dagger striper to make fine striper
10. Spool of heavy black thread for winding and tying hairs to handle
11. Completed hairline striper with wound thread tied in double knot
12. Heavy quill striper for wide gold and semi-transparent stripes on yellow furniture
13. Smaller quill striper for lines heavier than hair striper
14. Special cardboard brush made for curly maple grain striping on painted flat buff background. See page 17.

8

Dark Blue: one pint cans used in coach painting and now on chests and mixed with white for blue tints.

Lamp Black: half pint cans, quarts and tubes, the standard graining medium when thinned with japan drier and/or with turpentine.

ARTISTS' COLORS IN OIL (TUBES)

Used always where a transparent, shading color is needed, or for superimposing or overlay on gold leaf and stenciling.

> Alizarin Crimson
> Crimson Lake
> Gamboge or Yellow Lake
> Prussian Blue
> Verdigris
> Mauve

Opaque Oil Colors in Tubes
> Phillip's White
> Lamp Black or Ivory Black
> Yellow Ochre
> *Burnt Sienna*
> Burnt Umber
> *Raw Umber*

MATERIALS REQUIRED FOR WORK OTHER THAN PAINTS.

> *1 quart standard paint remover*
> *Scraper or steel square scraper*
> No. 2 steel wool, 1 pound
> *No. 00 steel wool, 1 pound*
> *No. 1 steel wool, 1 pound*
> *1 quart gum turpentine*
> *1 quart wood or denatured alcohol*
> *2 tack cloths — lintless (very necessary)*
> *Sandpaper No. 1 and No. ½, No. 4/0 garnet sandpaper*
> Small can plastic wood
> *1 quart best grade (5 pound cut) orange shellac*
> *1 pint high quality furniture varnish*
> *1 pint walnut varnish stain*
> 1 pint dark oak varnish stain
> *1 pint rubbed effect or satin varnish (if you so finish your furniture)*
> 1 quart flat white paint
> 1 quart paraffine oil
> 1 pound Italian pumice stone (medium)
> *Bottle gold size*
> *1 book (24 leaves) transfer gold leaf*
> *Bronze powders (detailed in Chapter III)*
> Etching tool
> Chalk or powdered lithopone

MATERIALS FOR TRACING AND STENCIL CUTTING.

> *½ yard traceolene or acetate tracing paper*
> *1 yard of architect's tracing linen or ten sheets already cut size 11 inches by 8½ inches*
> 1 No. 11 Exacto stencil knife, or
> *six single edge razor blades*
> *Square of window glass 9 inches by 12 inches*
> Good quality small oil stone
> *Scotch tape*
> *Piece of velour or velvet for bronze powder palette*
> *Square of very fine weave wool for making "bobs"*
> Spool of heavy black thread
> 3 penholders, cut in half.

Antique Color Recipes

For touching up chairs that are worn in spots where the old decorations must be preserved.

ANTIQUE RED

1. To two tablespoons of permanent vermilion (ground in japan) add smaller amounts of burnt umber, either japan or oil color. Thin this mixture with turpentine until it is light cream consistency. If the red is a more yellow tone, add very small amount of chrome yellow medium. There are many shades of antique red, but most of them have an initial base of the old American vermilion. If the old color is badly faded, add a touch of flat white.

ANTIQUE BLACK

2. Almost all old blacks are faded and of a greenish cast. To ½ pint japan black add 1 tube of raw umber mixed thoroughly in a larger can, and thinned with turpentine. Stir this well, and if the black is not yet green enough, add a small amount of chrome yellow medium. If the black has a brownish cast the mixture can be reddened by adding a little burnt Sienna.

ANTIQUE BROWN

3. Into a larger can put ½ pint japan black, to this add enough Venetian or Tuscan red (ground in japan) to make a rich brown. Thin to cream consistency with turpentine. If the brown is to be more golden add a small amount of chrome yellow medium, and an equal amount of raw Sienna.

ANTIQUE YELLOW

4. Place a pint can of flat white, after stirring, in a larger can. In the empty can put ½ tube chrome yellow medium (japan color), ½ tube of burnt umber (in oil) and one teaspoon of Prussian

blue. Mix these together thoroughly with a small amount of turpentine. Add the mixture to the white in larger can and thin to brushing consistency with turpentine. All old yellows were on the greenish tone and will dry one or two shades darker than the color in the can.

ANTIQUE GREEN

5. There is no more pleasing color for certain chairs, which was used long before 1800, than a soft antique green. The exact color is hard to match today. The most outstanding example of this early color is in the Henry duPont museum, *Winterthur*, at Wilmington, Delaware. In the eighteenth century kitchen are a set of Windsor chairs, some Sheraton Combback Windsors with scroll "ears," and some armed, nine spindle hoopback Windsors. They are painted in this lovely old coachpainter's green. It can be almost matched today by mixing ½ pint can of Willey's chrome green light with a little less than half this amount of burnt umber (japan color) and thinning with turpentine after pouring in a larger can. Add the umber gradually and never enough to "kill" the original clear green color. Always varnish over this green with two coats of satin varnish for wearing qualities.

ANTIQUE STENCILED MIRROR
INSIDE BORDER GOLD LEAF
Courtesy Campbell-Whittlesy House, Landmark Society, Rochester, N. Y.

STENCILING AND GOLD LEAF ON PEDESTAL
OF OLD MAHOGANY TABLE
Courtesy Campbell-Whittlesy House, Rochester, N. Y.

10

CHAPTER III

*An hour's industry will do more to produce cheerfulness, suppress
evil humors and retrieve your affairs than a month's moaning.*

BENJAMIN FRANKLIN

INSTRUCTIONS FOR PAINTING AND GRAINING ON OLD CHAIRS OR THEIR REPRODUCTIONS

First Project

The Attic Chair is good practice for beginning in stenciling. By an "attic chair" we mean one that has many old coats of paint or has not been touched for years. We know only too well that the beginner in this stencil hobby is anxious to make a fine show-ing on an interesting chair at the earliest possible moment. You may have found an interesting Sheraton Fancy chair or a Hitchcock in an antique shop or at an auction. The temptation is strong to start right in on this good piece. It is wiser to "creep" a little before you walk. Try an easy piece first. Up in the attic you undoubtedly will find a nondescript family chair, maybe a pair. Let's call it our "attic chair," just the thing to practice on. Nine times out of ten the original decoration, if any, is under five or more coats of paint.

Stripping

Removing varnish and heavy coats of paint, known as stripping the chair or "taking down." Obtain a quart of standard paint remover. Avoid inhaling fumes in summer by stripping in the shade out of doors; in winter, in cellar away from any medium of heat.

1. Put on rubber gloves to protect hands. Pour remover into open container, a coffee can, for example. With old paint brush, put a thick coat on a small section of chair. Wait until remover has "worked" on the paint and it can be crackled. With putty knife or old dull kitchen knife, scrape off what will come off easily. For rungs and turnings, use pad of No. 1 or No. 2 steel wool dipped in the remover and *scrubbed around* the turnings. If old paint comes off only in top layers, apply another coat of remover and continue this stripping until down to the bare wood. A new remover is on the market, without wax base, called NO-WASH REMOVER, which is powerful and leaves no residue. It needs no turpentine as a neutralizer.

2. Dip a piece of No. 1 steel wool in turpentine and rub chair thoroughly. This is a twofold opera-tion, smoothing and neutralizing remover at the same time.

3. When chair is thoroughly dry, sand carefully with No. 0 sandpaper and rub with No. 1 steel wool on turnings and rungs. Chair is ready now for background coat of paint. Next painting step on Attic Chair is taken up on page 14.

Second Project

UNCOVERING OLD DESIGNS

1. Old chairs without many coats of paint may still have original decoration, perhaps faded or hidden. Dip a cloth in wood or denatured alcohol and rub furniture, in area of design. Rub carefully. Design will appear brighter and brighter as old shellac finish is soluble in alcohol. Maybe you have a Boston rocker where the head rested on back splat and a film has formed over design. A small piece of No. 00 steel wool dipped in alcohol will get it down faster. Be careful not to take off design itself. When design seems to be as bright as it will be, let one coat of tacky shellac dry hard.

TRACING OLD DESIGN

2. Cut a piece of traceolene or frosted acetate the size of the design panel. Attach it firmly to chair with Scotch tape, as slipping will make the tracing inaccurate. Then with very sharp medium-hard pencil carefully trace off every detail of de-sign. Some prefer India ink for this tracing, but pencil is less trouble and it can be inked in later for a permanent record. Shadings can be made easier with pencil right over traceolene. Pens are usually advocated for tracing directly on tracing cloth. However, this is very seldom transparent enough to see through to old design.

Formerly, before acetate was obtainable, we used thin tracing paper which was made more transparent by varnishing one side and applying this side to the pattern to be traced, smoothing it down carefully with a cloth to get a tight contact. When tracing and shading were accurately recorded, it was lifted off, varnish wiped carefully from the back with clean cloth and set aside to dry. Trace-olene has greatly improved this old method. In restoring antique Hitchcocks, etc., where only chair rungs and legs are worn, it is not necessary to remove original coat of shellac. Merely sandpaper where worn or where old finish is rough and then touch up in worn spots and faded decorations.

METHOD OF FINDING DESIGN UNDER HEAVY COATS OF PAINT

3. Do not start scraping the back panel or places where designs might be. To find this hidden treasure, if at all valuable, is a tiring process. All thick paint may have proved a blessing in having preserved a fine design intact for a hundred years or more. Anyway, the anticipation is often worth the effort.

Dip a piece of 00 steel wool in paint remover. The outside enamel will come off readily. The undercoats will be harder, for the old paint was a zinc mixture. Work very carefully where the design should be, using a cloth dipped in denatured alcohol as you approach the design. If you are careful, the original design will gradually become visible. It is better to work down where the center of design might be. You can then quickly tell if it is worth while. If not, there is no point in removing the paint at the edges of the panel.

OLD DESIGNS WORTH DISCOVERING

4. You may uncover a rare old pattern which is certainly well worth the effort. In 1932, on a fine set of Sheraton Fancy chairs we found an exquisite gold-leaf eagle put on probably soon after the Revolution. The eagle was beautifully shaded with umber; the feathers distinct with the finest black brush lines. See illustration, page 113. The chairs proved to be painted originally a very pink ivory with wide gold-leaf stripes and fine dark red striping. These were restored as original. If great care had not been taken to find the eagle and stripes it would have been impossible to restore the set authentically. This is the only time on the many thousands of restored chairs that we found this same eagle done by a very early expert craftsman.

Repair Chairs before Painting

1. If furniture is shaky, have it reglued by a carpenter or cabinetmaker. This expert will knock the chair entirely apart and properly glue each section and reassemble with clamps. It is better to use an expert, unless you have a member of the family with experience in regluing furniture. Old chairs were put together without glue. Their rungs and stretchers were carefully dried; legs and backposts were "green" wood, not dried. As the "green" wood shrank, it gripped the rungs and back panel tighter and tighter.

2. Do not glue unless chair is very wobbly. If the rush or "flag" seat, made from cat-o'-nine-tails expertly woven by hand, needs replacing, there are workmen who are expert at a reasonable price. The same thing applies if the cane seat needs renewing. A new rush or cane seat oftentimes will "pull together" and so strengthen a slightly wobbly chair without regluing.

3. If the chair or piece is not too rough, and has only the original finish worn down in places, often it is necessary only to sand down carefully with No. ½ sandpaper, any rough spots with No. 1 sandpaper and finish off with No. 0 sandpaper. *Never sandpaper against the grain.* No. 1 steel wool is effective on the rungs and scrubbed *across* the length of the legs and around the turnings.

Painting

The chair, if properly sanded, is now ready to paint. Today some experts advocate a thin coat of diluted white shellac as a sealer.

No Sealer

We prefer to *let the undercoat act more as a stain,* sinking into the wood and making a closer bond with the old finish. Of course, if the chair is open grained oak, one or two coats of diluted shellac are necessary to seal the grain. There are several schools of conflicting opinion regarding sealing unpainted wood. We prefer *NO SEALER.*

OLD CHAIR FINISHES

Except for colored painted furniture, most of the old chairs, bureaus, washstands, etc., were finished to imitate the expensive rosewood. This was accomplished by one of five standard methods, the first method being by far the easiest and most universal.

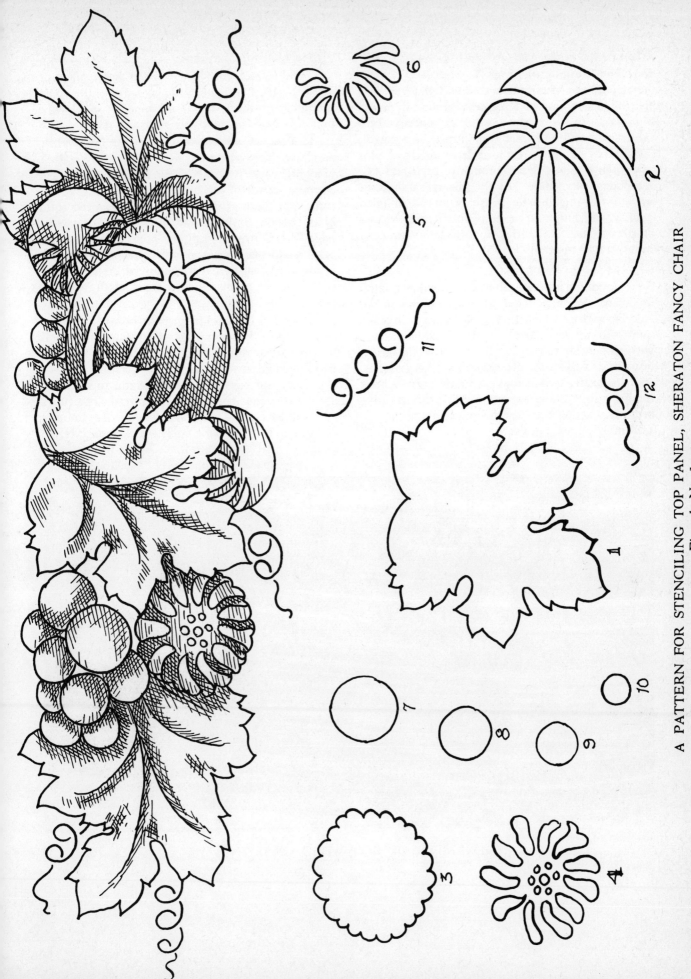

A PATTERN FOR STENCILING TOP PANEL, SHERATON FANCY CHAIR

First do No. 1, etc.

FIRST METHOD OF GRAINING

Rosewood Graining

1. Paint the chair a base coat with flat Venetian red, which is about 80% pigment, ground in japan, obtainable in ½ pint cans. Put contents into larger can, and with real gum turpentine, thin to consistency of light cream. Stir in about ½ pint of turpentine long and thoroughly, then add five teaspoons of varnish. Apply this red undercoat with a two-inch bristle brush or oxtail of good quality, brushing out carefully so no brush marks or runs show. This dries rapidly, but wait until the next day to grain.

Graining on the Red Base Coat

2. Graining is done with black flat paint, ground in japan. Some prefer drop black ground in oil. Add japan drier yourself. In either case, thin down more than the red undercoat. It should be thinned with turpentine so that it will drip from the brush into the can when the dipped brush is held over it. An inexpensive two-inch black bristle brush is good for graining. Some experts "pink" the graining brush by cutting out uneven scallops along the tip. This makes a good grain.

Method of Work

3. Sit comfortably in a low chair and do all your work the least fatiguing way by turning the chair around in front of you. You cannot do good work unless you concentrate with relaxed nerves.

4. Take off all excess black paint from brush and have the brush almost dry. Start with the back of a Hitchcock chair or rocker. Draw the brush the *complete* length of the back panel, starting at the top. The decorated front panel is painted solid black to show up the design better. See illustration, page 73. Continue until the panel is all grained. Start next at the very top of the side posts or stiles. Draw the brush the entire length of the post. Do the same on the sides and front of the stile or post.

Next grain pillow or grip or bolster top, the entire length, being careful to get the black down between the turnings properly, so that no plain red will show up between the high spots. Do the front legs and front stretcher, being careful to have the grain continuous between the turnings. The rungs are grained along their *entire* length. In graining the spindles of a Boston rocker it adds interest to

EXAMPLE OF ROSEWOOD GRAINING

14

wiggle the brush from side to side both back and front. When graining the plank or wooden seat of a rocker or side chair, grain the extreme curved back from left to right down to where the pieces are glued together. Start from this intersection and pull the brush toward you from back to front, going entirely over the front roll to the bottom in one continuous grain. In the center of plank seats the old workmen often wiggled the brush to make an interesting grain.

5. Grain each section of a chair as a unit entirely before going to the next part. The grain should always run the length of a part as it would in the natural wood. In graining bureaus, tables, etc., run the grain the entire length of the top or bureau drawer the width of the brush again and again until the entire surface has an even homogeneous grain.

Brush versus a Wad

6. There have been many advocates of painting a chair all black over the red undercoat and wiping off the black in places to simulate grain with cheesecloth, crumpled newspapers, cloth netting or anything handy. Maybe the old workmen did this. It would be hard to prove one way or another, but certainly, of the thousands we have examined and done over, all the best early chairs had a definite *brush or feather* grain. In the late decadent period they did almost anything, and some of these may have been done by the crumpled hit or miss method. At least the cloth method is rough on the hands, and this alone would throw it out for any craftsman. After experimenting we found the nearest approach to the old method was obtained by an *application of walnut varnish stain* the day after graining. We have never been satisfied with the use of clear varnish colored with raw umber, burnt umber or raw Sienna as a means of mellowing the regular rosewood graining. The results are inferior and cloudy. We prefer the walnut varnish as mentioned.

7. Apply a thin coat of walnut varnish stain evenly over the grained chair. If you want the grain to show redder, use dark oak *varnish* stain. This greatly improves the wearing qualities and necessitates fewer final coats for a proper finish. After the chair is thoroughly dry the next day, rub down all over carefully with No. 1 steel wool, and it is then ready for decoration. Wipe meticulously with your tack cloth.

SECOND METHOD OF GRAINING

Red Hairline or Feather Graining

Usually found on Hitchcock chairs; sometimes on Boston rockers.

1. The chair is painted entirely flat black (black ground in japan or drop black, thinned with turpentine and japan drier added) three tablespoons of varnish to a pint of paint.

2. The graining is done with a turkey feather, trimmed one inch wide with a scissors. The feather is dipped in a mixture of English or American vermilion diluted very thin with turpentine. The feather, wet with paint, is drawn on its side along the back panel and down the stiles. This leaves a few fine red lines, giving the general effect of a black chair. While this method is early, authentic, and often used on Hitchcocks, it has not that depth of finish of the regular rosewood grain. It seems to be primarily a speed-up process, and we suspect done originally because the brush graining must be more expertly done. This method, of course, obviates the need of the mellowing walnut varnish stain, and thus time is saved.

THIRD METHOD OF GRAINING

Brown Graining

Expert drawn walnut graining is found on the best early Cornucopia chairs, sometimes on adapted type Hitchcock chairs, on Duncan Phyfe type chairs and quite often on Boston rockers with cane seats. The graining was done with a brush usually "pinked," dipped in very thin antique black, and grained on the raw maple or pine wood. On the wide surfaces the beautiful grain was made often with iron or wooden combs. The process is so expert that it is not advocated for the amateur. It can be done today, however, with a "pinked" brush.

1. Clean chair thoroughly to bare wood and sand it much more carefully than for graining method I or II, using No. 1 steel wool around the turnings to have them perfectly smooth.

2. Mix ½ pint can of burnt umber in japan as for Venetian red undercoat, but considerably thinner. If too brown, add a small amount of flat black. This will make a real Van Dyke brown. Dip brush in graining paint and draw over newspapers to get it drier. Grain back panel, starting at left exactly where panel intersects stile. Great care must be taken to have brush come clear to intersection of back panel and right-hand poster

stile. Any mistakes or lifting of the brush from the surface will show up vividly, and on the raw maple cannot be erased or taken off. With this brown mixture, stencil panel was usually grained and not painted solid black. Until you become proficient in graining, it is better to practice for some time on a smooth pine board to get the "feel" of the brush, using *always* the *tip of* bristles only.

3. After the piece is grained to your satisfaction, working section by section, let dry for one day. The next day, to blend the contrasting grain, put over the entire chair a thin coat of dark oak varnish stain. If the grain does not tone down properly, put on a second coat of the oak stain the next day. Again, if you add raw Sienna and burnt umber to clear varnish you may "muddy" the grain too much. The ready mixed oak stain is much more transparent. You may find that ½ walnut varnish stain and ½ oak will give proper depth faster than two coats of oak. Experiment a little. When the varnish stain is thoroughly dry, rub down with No. 0 steel wool before stenciling or applying gold leaf on grained panels and side posts. For stenciling directions and striping, see Chapters V and VI.

FOURTH METHOD OF GRAINING
Sometimes Called Tortoise Shell Graining

Tortoise shell graining is effective on fine Sheraton chairs. Used on chairs, the effect is similar to earlier graining on "floor" of painted trays. A crude form of this graining was often used on the later mass production of settees, hooded cradles and two-tiered washstands.

PREPARATION

1. After cleaning paint from chair, paint it a little brighter red than for rosewood grain. This is made with ⅔ Venetian red and ⅓ permanent vermilion, both japan colors, purchased in ½ pint cans. Thin with turpentine and add two tablespoons of varnish.

Black Used to Grain on Red Undercoat

2. After chair is thoroughly dry, using same thin black japan color thinned with turpentine, somewhat thinner than for brush graining, apply black as follows.

APPLICATION

3. Dip a small sponge, piece of wadded paper napkin or cotton cloth in saucer of the black mixture, pat on piece of newspaper to remove excess.

Start with back of top back panel of your Sheraton chair, *stipple* with uneven *blob* effect. Allow much more red to show than in brush rosewood grains. The sponge or napkin crumpled is not drawn along the red undercoat, but patted on. A little practice will give an interesting effect. The black should have the effect of a superimposed film or web over the red. Pat the black over the entire chair in the following order: back of top splat, the stiles, front and back each side, front or decorated part of top splat, the front legs all around, the rungs, and, if the seat is wooden or plank, do this last with the veiled uneven *blob* effect with much red showing.

A Glaze Over the Blob Grain

4. When thoroughly dry, "pull" the whole effect together with a thin coat of light oak varnish stain. If, when this is dry, the effect is not antique looking enough, give it a second coat of the oak stain. This stain is very transparent, and if a more subdued effect is desired, add ¼ tube, size 2, raw Sienna and ¼ gamboge (oil colors) to one pint clear varnish. Never add enough of the colors to make the effect muddy.

THE FIFTH METHOD
Graining to Imitate Curly Maple

This is the only light-colored grain used by the early craftsmen. It was, when well done, a marvelous imitation of curly maple, usually reserved only for the finer Sheraton chairs, sometimes a more elaborate broken arch top washstand and other well-made pieces. We have done much of this tedious graining on entire sets of Sheraton chairs. If you have a particularly good chair, and want it to blend with other maple pieces in your room, there is nothing better than this maple grain decorated with gold leaf.

METHOD OF PREPARATION

1. Clean chair thoroughly with paint remover as stipulated for rosewood. Sandpaper thoroughly, and apply a thin coat of white or orange shellac. Any unevenness will show up more on this grain than on darker finishes. Holes should be puttied up carefully with common white putty and sanded smoothly.

2. Paint the chair a light buff color. This is made by pouring one pint of flat white, thoroughly mixed and thinned to cream consistency, into a larger can. Into the empty pint can squeeze ½ large tube of raw umber ground in oil; to this add

about one tablespoon of the japan Venetian red used in undercoat. You are trying to get the light buff color of old maple wood, and may need a dash of chrome yellow medium. Stir this mixture with a little turpentine thoroughly in the pint can. Pour this color into the flat white and stir thoroughly. If too thick, thin with turpentine so no brush marks will show. With a good two-inch brush apply an even coat over the entire chair as outlined in Chapter III.

Hunt around a little in the paint stores. You may find a ready mixed light buff paint that will do nicely, but it is better to thin this somewhat with turpentine. Next day, when thoroughly dry, the chair will be ready for the curly grain, after you have sanded the larger panels lightly with No. 00 sandpaper.

MATERIALS FOR CURLY MAPLE GRAINING

The Brush; The Grain Compound

1. The brush for this graining must be specially made by yourself. Obtain six small round inexpensive water-color brushes in six sizes from the smallest to size six. These may or may not be camel's-hair. Cut the brush handles in half. Take two stiff pieces of cardboard three inches square; glue the six brush handles to the bottom cardboard. A good cardboard is made from corrugated box with the brush handles glued into six grooves. Put glue along top of handles and press the upper cardboard firmly down with a weight.

The metal ferules should project beyond the cardboard. When the glue is dry, with a heavy black thread and large needle sew back and forth through both cardboards, securing the brush handles tightly. See sketch on page 8.

2. Next, the graining compound is made as follows. In ½ pint can mix ½ small tube of raw umber, add one teaspoonful of the Venetian red undercoat thinned with turpentine to milk consistency. The color should resemble the color of thinned orange shellac. Some of these old Sheratons were actually grained with thin orange shellac.

Do not get this graining color too dark, the contrast will be too great. If too dark, add some thinned flat white paint.

Graining the Curly Maple Stripes

3. Dip your graduated six point brush in the graining mixture, remove excess on newspapers. At extreme left side of back panel draw the grain down perpendicular to the slat. Continue working the full length of the slat. The curly marks will automatically space themselves. Do this next on the strip on the back of the seat. Take each section of chair and finish it entirely before going to the next. On the stiles or posts, the legs, and the rungs the brush is pulled completely around the stile or leg, and some care should be taken to have the six varying lines meet properly. If the lines wiggle a bit it will look all the more like curly maple.

4. To pull this decided grain together with the buff undercoat, next give the chair a smooth even coat of dark oak varnish stain, thinned. If it seems too dark, add thinned clear varnish and sometimes a bit of raw umber to gain a more golden look. The chair is decorated after this coat is thoroughly dry. If you have worked carefully, the effect definitely resembles a curly maple chair.

Finish the chair with thin shellac or satin varnish.

Smoky Effect Backgrounds

Used on bellows and occasionally Sheraton Fancy chairs. On a very few expensive Sheraton chairs and a great many turtleback bellows the mottled smoke background was used.

1. Paint the chair or bellows with flat white paint and wait until next day when dry, when you can give it a thin coat of clear varnish and "hold" the smoke or carbon deposit.

2. Hold the bellows or chair over a smoky candle, moving it not too close so that the black is deposited on the tacky varnish in a marbleized effect. Have the marbleizing in an interesting pattern of a uniform cloudiness with no deep contrasting black spots.

3. Next day varnish the entire article to hold the effect and to preserve it.

HAND-PAINTED TOP PANEL, EARLY ARROWBACK CHAIR

A PRACTICE PROJECT

This unusual design was found on a set of very early arrowback chairs painted a rich tobacco brown.

PROCEDURE

1. Trace the design, page 18, in its entirety on good quality traceolene.

2. If you have one arrowback chair or a set, or perhaps a *wide top panel* other type of early chair, paint it a deep rich brown. This can be made from ½ pint (japan color) burnt Sienna to which is added a small amount of japan black and a dash of chrome yellow medium, all thinned to brush out evenly with gum turpentine. Paint your piece two coats, sanding between, 48 hours apart.

3. When thoroughly dry, with a chalked or lithopone tracing paper under your traceolene pattern, trace the outline only of the design on the chair panel. Trace also the heavy black brush strokes. Do the same with the design on the arrows if an arrowback.

4. For the buds and central poppy paint in with American or permanent vermilion the outside petals and bud tips. Blend these darker to the bases with crimson lake or alizarin crimson (oil color in tube).

5. Next paint in with a sage or olive green the leaves and the bud and poppy bracts, darkening the green with a dash of black towards the center of the two leaves. The top brush stroke motif on the arrow is this same outer leaf green; the lower brush stroke on arrow is the deeper poppy red.

6. Two days later, when these painted-in portions are entirely dry, mix a soft mustard yellow and brush in with your small flat tipped red sable brush the heavy black brush strokes around the poppy and leaves. With your finest pointed watercolor brush put in all the hairline strokes in this yellow as indicated. Also superimpose the same yellow on the brush strokes on the red and green heavy strokes on the arrows.

7. The painting is finished, except for the stamens and fine lines on center of the poppy, which are in this japan black.

8. When thoroughly dry, varnish the panel and arrows, stripe with mustard yellow the rest of the chair and in 24 hours give the chair a coat of satin finish varnish, with a second coat the next day. You now have a decorated piece with a rare early design which we found originally in 1937.

CHAPTER IV

True happiness comes to him who does his work well,
followed by a relaxing and refreshing period of rest.

LIN YUTANG

CUTTING THE STENCIL. MATERIALS AND PROCEDURE

Tracing the Decoration

1. If you have traced the stenciled design from your old chair or from this book onto the acetate paper, or a traceolene, you are now ready to transfer it to the stencil material.

Material for Making Stencils

2. All old stencils were cut from various grades of paper, sometimes oiled. Today all authorities agree that tracing cloth or architect's linen is the proper material for stencils. One of its advantages being transparency over the tacky varnish, you can see the already stenciled units and get more accurate positions. If properly used, this cloth lasts indefinitely. When the stencils become gummy with varnish, we clean them with paint remover and wipe off carefully, then iron to make them flat. Place creased stencil between newspapers and press with warm iron. *No moisture or water* must ever touch this cloth, as it will quickly ruin your cut stencil.

Tight Contact Between Stencil and Varnished Surface Essential to Stenciling

3. The contact made by linen and tacky varnish is ideal; it is less apt to slip than paper stencils. The tracing cloth can be purchased in *different widths* and cut to proper size.

LOOSELEAF NOTEBOOK SIZE READY-CUT IS AUTHOR'S ORIGINAL IDEA

4. Or we buy a dozen sheets of tracing cloth *notebook size* 11 by 8½", with three holes which make it easy to keep your cut stencils in a regular 9 x 12" looseleaf notebook between alternating sheets of notebook paper. You have your master tracing taken from your chair or from some design in this book. You must now "break down" the

SPECIMEN SAMPLE AUTHOR'S STENCIL, SIZE 8½ BY 11"

design into the individual units, far enough apart on the 11 x 8½" sheet so that in stenciling they will be easy to put the bronzes through without registering the next unit on the varnish. It will also help greatly if you will place the traced units on the linen in the same general position as on the traced master design. See page 31 for a notebook sheet of a chair stencil.

It is handier to have units on one sheet than on separate pieces. Time lost in hunting a stencil at the critical stage of varnish "tackiness" may result in necessity for revarnishing — never very satisfactory.

Cutting Instrument

5. There is considerable diversity of opinion as to what is used to cut a stencil. Many use nail, embroidery or cuticle scissors with success. The old experts used nothing but a well-sharpened stencil knife, pressed down hard on newspapers, a pine board, or, preferably, a piece of tin. We, long years ago, learned to manipulate adroitly a single edge razor blade, cutting on a piece of glass. See illustration below. Hold the razor blade very tightly in the right hand (if right handed) and manipulate or *rotate* the cloth sheet with the left hand. If there are many dots or *small circles* in the design, always cut these *first*.

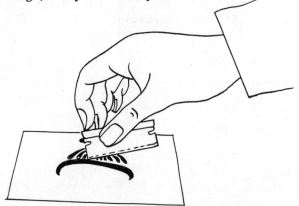

CUTTING STENCIL WITH SINGLE EDGE BLADE
Pressure applied with forefinger

Then cut the finer openings and the hairlines, cutting from the center of a large one-piece stencil to the outer openings. The finest hairlines can be cut readily, like the line around half of a peach, with the razor blade with no deviation in thickness. We have found it impossible to cut with a scissors fine hairlines of uniform width. After all the units are cut out accurately, with fine sharp lines, your cut stencil is ready to apply on the "tacky" varnish and to shade with the larger *bobs* the different bronzes through the cut openings.

Just this final note on cutting minute and larger circles. The old experts used various sized punches. With practice, just as accurate a minute circle can be cut with the razor blade if it is held *firmly* in the right hand and the tracing cloth *rotated* with the left hand. As soon as the blade shows dullness, both ends having been used, throw it away and take another. See picture of one-piece fiddleback stencil, page 98.

Care of Stencils

Stencils, if broken, can be repaired with Scotch tape.

After each contact with bronze powder, stencil should be wiped clean with paint remover, Carbona, or a cleaning fluid.

When first cutting out stencil, try to allow a margin of *one inch* all around a single motif, so that when powders, etc., are being applied, they will not mess up adjoining motif.

When tracing for a stencil, do not copy lettering, guide signs or instructional words. Also, do not copy crosshatching in our stencils, as they are guides for shading.

CENTER PANEL DECORATION FOR BOSTON ROCKER BUILT-UP STENCIL
FOR FRUIT GROUP

A PRACTICE PROJECT

The sketches on page 22 now show the order of "building up" the fruit units to a completed pattern. Starting with pineapple base unit No. 1, the main unit No. 2 fades into and is partly hidden by unit No. 1 or the stem section.

Melon unit No. 3 is partly obscured by the right side of the pineapple.

Peach unit put on next is very slightly hidden by the left side of pineapple unit 2.

Flower unit No. 5 is made effective because it comes *over* peach at the lower left part and hides *behind* the pineapple at its lower right. While this unit No. 5 was stenciled on *after* unit No. 4, it has what is called the "double effect" stenciling, i.e., part of unit overlapping another and part of same unit hiding behind another unit.

Used extensively in old stenciling, it entirely took away the *flat* effect and seemed to give the flower a natural contour.

Leaf unit No. 6 next stenciled is very slightly hidden and is shaded, as is No. 7 leaf, with a separate piece of cut-out curved linen.

The final drawing showing all the assembled units through No. 11 indicates how depth and interest are created by having the last applied leaves or "feathering-out" units appear, some in front and some hiding behind the previously stenciled main units. This illusion of contour for each unit applied was the secret of the effectiveness of the early stenciling and appears entirely lost in the late mass production period of furniture decoration.

STEP-BY-STEP PROCESS IN BUILDING UP A MULTIPLE STENCIL

EARLY STENCILED LEAF AND GRAPE DESIGN WITH FREEHAND YELLOW VEINS AND UNUSUAL SCROLLS

ANOTHER PRACTICE PROJECT

This is an arrowback or wide board top thumb-back chair design, dating well before 1830. It is the largest and one of the most graceful grape leaves we have yet found stenciled.

Procedure

a. Trace the entire design on your traceolene or acetate paper, except for the crosshatched shading which is only to indicate how the bronze powder is shaded.

b. Over your tracing lay a piece of architect's linen, and trace on this the *outline* only of the leaf. The turned-up tip of leaf is a separate unit to cut out. Trace three sizes of circles as indicated to be cut out for three sizes of grapes. That gives you *five different units* to cut out for stencils from the linen.

c. Prepare your chair with the rosewood finish as detailed on page 14. If you prefer, the chair can be done in the soft old green as detailed under "colors," page 7. If you use green, the outlines of the design will have to be traced on the panel and filled in with flat black paint as done for the yellow thumbback chair, Work Pattern No. 1.

d. You have cut from linen five units as indicated above. Varnish your back panel and when the right tackiness, stencil with No. 65 (Both) bright gold, working next to darker gold, well blended and fading off rapidly with statuary bronze to the dark center of leaf. The crosshatching will guide your shading. Next, stencil the bottom turned-up cut-out in silver powder.

e. In shading the grapes, start at the top left hand with the bright gold powder and fade with deeper gold to the bottom of each grape.

f. What will lift your grape shading right out of the amateur class is the following step: after all the grapes are shaded as indicated above and in the sketch with the crosshatch lines, take your small chamois *bob*, dip it in your silver powder, then, on newspapers and with a rapid *circular* motion, make a highlight on each grape about where the black dot appears in the sketch.

g. The stenciling must dry overnight. Wash off with water the next day, wipe dry and give the panel a coat of clear furniture varnish. This is expedient, for if any mistakes are made with the yellow veins and scrolls they can be wiped off without spoiling the stencil.

h. When varnish is very dry next day, with chalked paper under your traceolene, trace the yellow veins and scrolls with the yellow dot on each grape. Mix a soft mustard yellow (chrome yellow medium plus raw Sienna [oil color] plus a dash of japan black). Have the mixture fairly thin and add a few drops of varnish. Do *not* thin with turpentine. Use your smallest flat end red sable brush, and with a rapid whole arm movement brush in the veins, scrolls and dots on grapes as indicated. When quite dry, after striping your entire chair, wait 24 hours and give it two coats of satin varnish a day apart.

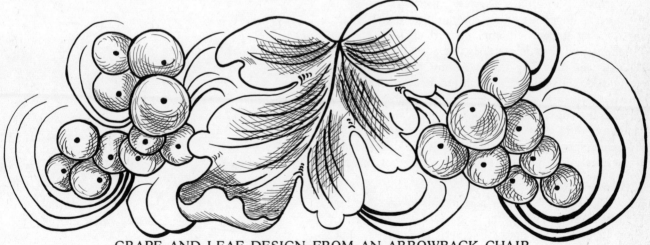

GRAPE AND LEAF DESIGN FROM AN ARROWBACK CHAIR
Reduced from nine inches

CHAPTER V

Joy dwells beneath a humble roof;
Heaven is not built of country seats
But little queer suburban streets.

CHRISTOPHER MORLEY

STENCILING WITH BRONZE POWDERS

Right and Wrong Varnishes

Chair has been prepared as instructed in Chapter III with the rubbed-down flat-looking walnut varnish stain. The parts to be stenciled are to be varnished with clear varnish applied evenly. Use a two-inch camel's-hair brush, which leaves no brush marks. The varnish for stenciling is *very* important. Most varnishes are made with an oil base. If you use a heavy waterproof varnish, made especially for floors, right out of the can, you will come to grief. It is altogether too heavy. A good *furniture varnish* is much superior and should be thinned by adding ¼ part pure turpentine poured into a saucer and mixed thoroughly. Do not stir the turpentine with the varnish in the can as the bubbles formed are hard to eradicate. By all means, avoid a "heavy body" varnish that dries slowly up to a certain point and then dries hard so quickly that you are unable to stencil the entire area with uniform brilliance.

Right Tackiness for Stenciling

1. In room temperature (70°), with the thinned varnish the proper "resist finger" tackiness is reached in about twenty minutes to a half hour. ("Resist finger" is point where it clicks — ever so slight pull, but finger does not actually stick.) If you wait too long the stenciling will be too pale and look anemic, even with increased pressure. If the varnish is too wet you cannot shade properly and the edges will look flaky and the whole surface heavy and uninteresting. With experience, the exact stage of "tackiness" to "take" the bronze properly will become merely a matter of routine

The Velvet Palette Box

2. An ideal palette is a flat fifty-cigarette box (saved since before the war) into the bottom of which is glued a piece of velvet. The cover is shut, keeping out dirt when not in use.

On this palette place at two-inch intervals ½ teaspoonful of the following bronzes:

The bronzes matching the old stenciling.

No. 65   Gold lining by Otto Both, pale lemon gold called green gold. Much more brilliant and lively than the brushed brass commonly used.

No. 104   Deep gold lining by Otto Both.

No. 501   Chrome lining or silver bronze, finer ground than aluminum but not quite as brilliant.

No. 31   A deep Roman gold by Otto Both; a very expensive and beautiful deep gold fine ground and lovely, used together with No. 65.

No. 42   Statuary bronze by Venus, deep dull and not showing its effect unless under thin coats of orange shellac.

No. 26   Red by Venus, not used except in colored stenciling and primarily for dusting lightly centers of flowers, etc.

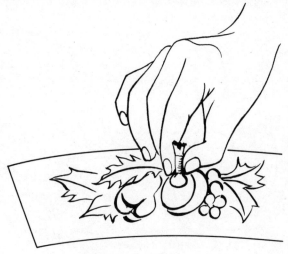

HOLDING THE BOB

24

The Bronze Powder Applicator

3. As early as 1775 metallic powders were used in stenciling trays in England and Wales. Designs like roses, certain fruits, and shells were stenciled through the cut-out pattern.

The highlights and fine interior shadings were put on freehand, when varnish was slightly drier, with small *bobs*.

Bob was the earliest name for the tool used in stenciling. *Bobs* were made in different sizes according to work to be done. A very small *bob* for extremely fine work. It was a small piece of *wool* wrapped around a tiny pad of cotton on a stick. The smallest *bobs* had no cotton padding. For the minute highlights and freehand *bob* work the effect gained was exactly like freehand dry brush work. For this a tiny piece of chamois or soft leather was drawn through a hollow quill, forming a tiny pad at the end.

Practice Project

4. Make five or six various size *bobs*. This expert manipulation of fine-pointed *bobs* is really, even today, the lost art of the pioneer craftsmen. No workman now can begin to approach these early geniuses, working years before 1800. The nearest approach seems to have been Gildersleeve about 1826–1830, active in New York on stenciled mahogany. Also, William Eaton, in his early work on shell manipulation, shows wonderful technique.

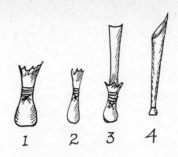

1. Fine wool cloth, cotton pad inside, tied with black thread.
2. Wool, tied with thread (no pad).
3. Chamois tied on stick.
4. Minute chamois pad pushed through hollow quill.

Bob versus Velvet Finger

These historical facts seem to contradict for all time the prevalent idea of the so-called "velvet finger." To begin with, the covered finger, index or otherwise, is too large and flat a medium for good shading, especially if the velvet should slip or become stuck to the varnish in places. Where the idea originated is problematical. The factory stencilers at Hitchcockville, Connecticut, used their bare index fingers, dipped first in oil, then in the bronze powder. The finger became like the olden day leather fire bucket.

PRACTICE IN SHADING LEAVES AND FRUIT

On page 49 is a group of fruit and leaves, two-toned to show approximately the effect of gold stenciling on a black surface. The central peach is the most used, a one-piece cut-out with left hairline outlining the shaded area. The three highlights of gold bronze are shown in shading the usual pear. The different sized circles show the usual individual grape shading on which the light is shown falling on the top left-hand side of the grape, with the largest grapes on the top and center and smaller grapes (circles) at the bottom.

All the leaves of different types and sizes are the early type shadings in which the midrib or veins are shaded by means of a separate curved piece of linen laid over the cut-out leaf. The *bob* loaded with the gold bronze is drawn along the curved small piece, fading the gold away from the sharply defined edge.

1. Trace on your architect's linen the outline of the peach, tracing *only the right cheek*, and the *extreme left hairline*, the parts to be cut out. Trace outline of pear on sheet some little space away from peach. Trace three sized circles for the three sized grapes. Next (spaced far enough apart not to interfere when the gold powder is put on the cloth), trace the outlines of large grape leaf, leaf above peach, and one of the small leaves underneath. Cut these units out as detailed, Chapter IV.

Practice on Cardboard

2. On a piece of *dry* cardboard, which you have *previously* painted flat black, put a thin coat of furniture varnish, smooth both ways evenly with your brush tip.

3. When it reaches proper tackiness, lay on the center peach, and taking the *bob*, well loaded with

gold powder No. 65 (Both) bright, draw the *bob* down along the curved right cheek, letting the gold fade out along the right-hand edge. Draw the *bob* along the left-hand cut-out hairline.

Lift the stencil, and with the *bob* well loaded, place it in the blank center of the peach. With a *round* and *round* circular motion of the *bob*, gradually approach the right cheek line and the left hairline, not taking more powder and fading into the background black.

The Pear

4. Place the pear cut-out in position and work it up about a quarter of the way, fading it out. Put more gold on the *bob*, and with circular motion shade the lower pear highlight. Do the same for the two highlights above, fading them out as in the illustration. Next, with a darker shade of bronze, run the *bob* along the left and right side of the pear cut-out.

Leaf Shadings

5. Lay the cut-out leaf corresponding to the illustration over the top of the peach so that it appears to hang over the darker shaded top of peach with a curved piece of linen extending from the point of the leaf to its base. Draw the *bob* along this curved line, letting the top of the gold shading fade away.

Some experts stroke in the edges of a leaf, leaving the dark center, lift their stencil, and with the curved linen piece shade the highlight midrib last.

We prefer to shade the midrib section *first* with the entire leaf cut-out firmly attached to the varnish, as there is less likelihood of the powder's flying too near the leaf edge and it can be controlled better.

We then draw the *bob* along the top and bottom edges of the leaf, then when the stencil is lifted, the entire leaf is done.

Place the small leaf cut-out on this right-hand side and shade this small leaf as done with the larger one over the top of the peach. Repeat this leaf four times, overlapping the leaves slightly so that one hides behind the other.

STENCILING BUNCH OF GRAPES

1. Start with the top grape, your largest circle. Fade the gold out at the bottom. Place the same circle slightly overlapping the first grape. From the bright gold top fade to the bottom of second grape. The third grape is the same circle as grapes 1 and 2. The next three grapes are the middle size and are shaded like this on top. The last two bottom grapes are the smallest circles. This method gives the bunch contour and makes it look natural.

The large leaves at left and right are shaded carefully with the curved linen, first the long ribs, then the shorter ones, which will give the leaf naturalness and character. *Master this little practice motif and you can adequately stencil almost any pattern.*

Although original Hitchcock settees are rare, they are available in reproductions. These copies of settees are available in plain, unfinished wood (white wood). Before decorating, see Chapters III and IV for preparation. With three identical sections to decorate, you will find this project offering a good opportunity to develop your skill in the essential decorative techniques: stenciling, shading, applying gold rings. See photo, page 30.

1. Measure the center of back panel of the three-part Hitchcock settee. Apply a thin coat of varnish as described under stencil varnish section.

Stenciling a Basket

2. Hold stencil sheet firmly on tacky varnish with center of basket exactly in center of panel.

Dip a large wool *bob* in silver powder, pat off excess on a piece of newspaper.

With a firm up and down motion, stencil through the center of the bowl from top to bottom of pedestal, making this the brightest highlight.

Dip again in silver powder and pat off most of it on newspaper. Then shade toward the edges of bowl on each side. This will give the illusion of a round bowl.

Lift stencil sheet carefully and with *bob* dipped in *deep* gold and patted off, make the highlight in center of bowl between the silver. Do not rub, but use quick motion from center to each side.

Stenciling and Shading a Peach

3. With this form of peach, which is the early round type you have, cut out only the right cheek and a very fine hairline that gives you the left limit of its size.

Place the right cheek of the peach at right side of basket so that it appears to be set *into* the basket. The *peach* is always stenciled with a little more *generous amount of powder* than for grapes and other fruit.

Dip a smaller sized *bob* in No. 65 (Both) pale lemon bronze, pat on paper and with stencil sheet held very firmly on varnished surface with left hand, bear down heavily with *bob* and stencil the right cheek and the hairline opposite side.

Lift up the stencil sheet carefully and place the central peach in the center of the basket, lower down in it to further the illusion of a round basket which *holds* fruit.

Stencil this right cheek and hairline, lift off sheet carefully and now shade the center of the two peaches. With a generous amount of No. 65 (Both) gold put the *bob* down on the center of the right peach and with a rapid pressure circular movement burnish the gold gradually, working towards the hairline and the right cheek without taking more powder.

If you want variation dip the *bob* in the deep gold and put most of the powder on the newspaper, and with same circular motion put on the deep gold, blending it with the center lighter gold, working toward the edges with no powder at all. The peach will then seem to be round and nicely shaded.

Next place the pear to left of center peach.

Stenciling and Shading a Pear

4. The pear has a special technique itself, consisting usually of three highlights; see illustration, page 49.

Pears usually contrast better with the peach if highlights are silver bronze. It is a matter of taste. Dip the *bob* in silver or No. 65 lemon gold with a generous amount and with the same circular pressure "round and round" movement, stencil the lower larger highlight, next the middle highlight above, and lastly the top highlight and stem with lesser bronze. Each with the circular motion graduated nicely in size.

Next dip the *bob* in the deep gold and with very little powder run it rapidly along the left-hand edge of the cut stencil and up the bottom, using care that the stencil sheet does not slip a hair.

Note: *This heavy pressure motion is the real secret of fine early stenciling. It works the powder into the varnish, burnishing at the same time. Many stencilers today "fluff" the powder onto the varnish with a patting motion; this quickly gets the powder out of control and gives an effect indecisive and "not quite sure of itself."*

The Midrib Shaded Leaf Technique

5. In this design, which we call our standard Hitchcock design, since it has all of the early technique with the long side leaves peculiar to Hitchcocks, add leaf No. 7, a peach leaf, over the center peach for interest.

MULTIPLE STENCIL DESIGN FOR HITCHCOCK CHAIR SPLAT

Reduced from original size of twelve and one-half inches

Full scale rose units, see page 140

28

WASHSTAND DECORATION, ORIGINAL DESIGN THIRTEEN INCHES

Poppy and leaf stenciled decoration, silver and gold powder combined with black brush strokes. Lined freehand brush strokes are in semi-transparent raw umber (raw umber mixed with varnish with a dash of burnt Sienna. This unusual decoration is adaptable to bureau drawers, rocker tops, dressing stands, etc., in yellow or rosewood. See photograph on page 34.

29

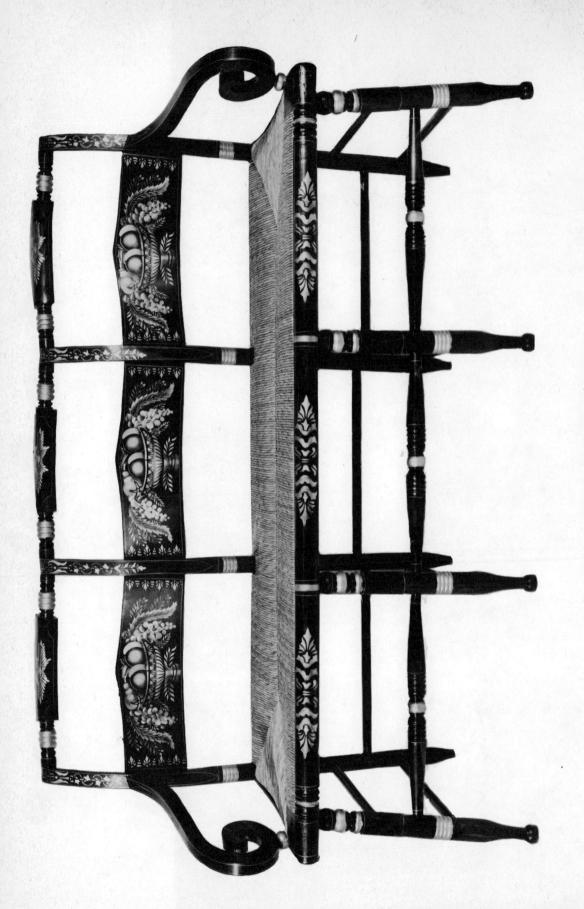

THREE-PART HITCHCOCK SETTEE

ALL STENCILED EXCEPT PILLOW BACK IN GOLD LEAF

See next page for fifteen separate stencil units. Front seat roll decoration same as on rockee,

Work Pattern 9

30

STENCIL UNITS FOR BOWL OR FRUIT GROUP ON BACK PANELS
OF THREE-IN-ONE HITCHCOCK SETTEE
See photo, page 30

STENCILED FRUIT GROUP FOR BOSTON ROCKER TOP PANEL
See page 22 for steps in building up this design

32

STENCILED DESIGN FOR TURTLEBACK HITCHCOCK CHAIR. See Work Pattern 5

33

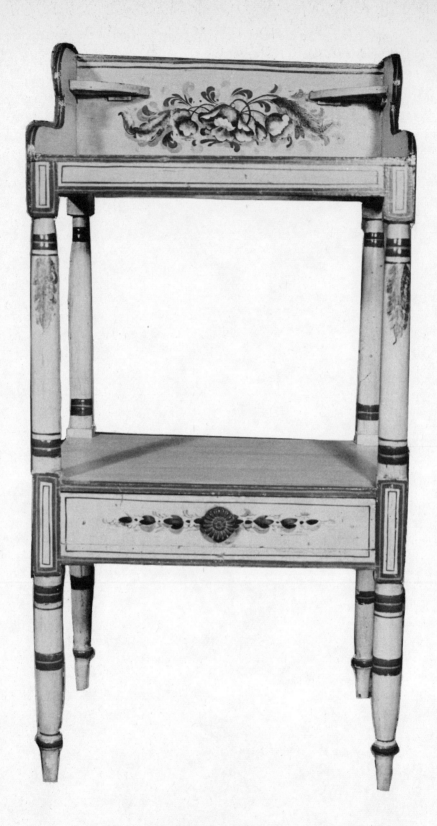

**YELLOW DECORATED WASHSTAND
SHERATON TYPE. ABOUT 1830**
Freehand brushwork on lower drawer and legs;
also on back and on back panel combined with
stenciling. See page 29 for details of top panel.

Place the leaf, and with a curved piece of tracing cloth down the middle of the leaf, draw the *bob* with No. 65 (Both) powder along this curved cut-out.

Then with the deep gold, draw it along the top of the cut-out leaf, shading toward the dark section above the curved cut-out.

Lift the curved piece and shade along bottom of leaf.

See illustrations on page 33, which show the leaf shading in actual size detail.

Grapes

6. Next put in the two bunches of grapes on each side of the dish. Start with the bottom grapes, with the sheet held very firmly to the varnish. Use copper or a deep gold bronze; for larger grapes, shade with No. 65 (Both) lemon gold, as if the light came from upper left-hand corner.

Now, to add interest, we shall superimpose the three sized cut-out circles: largest at the top of the bunch, medium near the middle of the bunch, and the smallest near the bottom in the open spaces, with some overlapping the one-piece cut-out bunch.

Always shade (with one of the very smallest *bobs*) the top side of the grape, fading it out to black near the bottom. This shading shows up nicely in the photograph on page 30.

Leaves

7. Next place the two elongated leaves either side of the grapes, drawing one of the larger *bobs* along the top of the leaf with pressure, No. 65 (Both) bronze, and the lower side of leaf, the deep gold or coppery bronze, leaving the center of the leaf dark.

Superimpose the cut-out veins exactly in the center of the right and the left leaf and stencil through the cut-out veins with silver bronze.

Stars

8. The four tiny star details are then put in each side of basket and above each bunch of grapes with silver.

Then the two leaf groups, Nos. 14 and 15, are put either side of the bowl stem and the feathering-out unit No. 13 is put in adjoining the two bottom stars and on the outside of each large leaf.

The panel is then stenciled except for the two side conventional motifs. This is done on a separate unit in statuary bronze as in drawing No. 1, thus fading away the whole design at the edges.

One-Piece Conventional Pattern on Stiles and Front Seat Roll

9. Put on front seat roll the same running border design used on pine chest, Work Pattern 8; now, after the varnish is the right tackiness, the stiles and front roll are stenciled with the largest *bob*, using No. 65 lemon bronze.

In stenciling the one-piece cut-outs, the varnish can be somewhat wetter than for the finely shaded panels.

In stenciling side posts, start with unit No. 1, page 136, of the cut-out stencil. With plenty of bronze, work with heavy pressure up to the top.

Hold the stencil unit very firmly with thumb and index finger, working the *bob*, always well loaded, up gradually to the top of your cut-out stencil. The stencil will not slip if held firmly with left hand.

The same procedure applies to the one-piece front roll unit. Start with the right-hand point, with the unit held firmly with the index and third finger at the edges of the curved roll, gradually working the *bob* in the right hand with pressure and plenty of bronze along with the two fingers as clamps toward the center of unit. Now you have the stenciling completed and only the conventional motif on the pillow, the gold rings and the striping remain to complete decoration.

Persevere

Don't be misled or discouraged by these elaborate stencil directions. It takes about one-third as long actually to stencil this back panel as it does to present it in this book.

An expert works like lightning, absolutely sure of himself. It all comes, of course, with practice

SIDE BORDER DESIGN FOR BACK PANELS, THREE-PART HITCHCOCK SETTEE

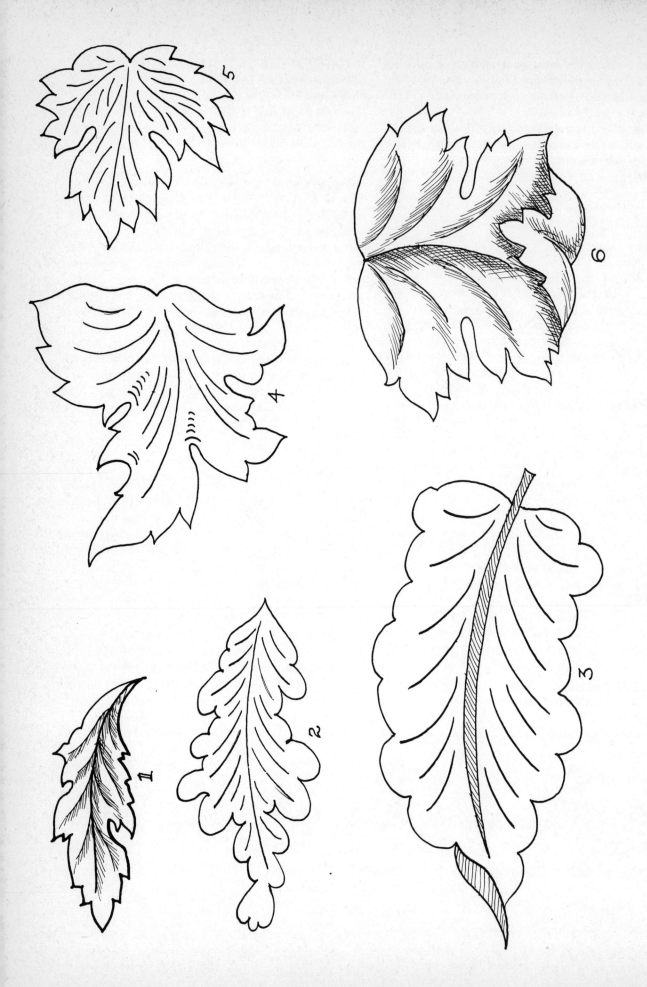

LEAF VARIANTS, SHOWING VEINING METHODS

36

and more practice. You would not expect to sit down at the piano and play Chopin's Etudes after your fifth music lesson. No more would you reasonably expect to do a perfect piece of stenciling on the first, second, or third chair. It will all come very easily, however, much more so, we can assure you, than Chopin after even three or four years of lessons.

Applying the Gold Rings

10. The better old chairs often had gold-leaf rings, sometimes the cheaper "Dutch Metal" leaf, a mixture of zinc and copper rolled slightly thicker than hand-hammered gold leaf. Today it is simpler to use a good lining bronze mixed with varnish with a slight amount of japan drier added.

a. Pour ½ spoonful No. 60 coach striping (Venus) bronze into a small can cover, add clear varnish and a few drops of drier to make it the consistency of thick cream.

b. Old chairs had rings on legs placed a little back of halfway around each side, rings on top posts and front rung, usually all around. This saves time, and when real gold is used, considerable gold leaf. Sit in a low chair, turn the chair around in front of you and do it the easy way.

Position for Stenciling

11. Least awkward way is to stand up, lay chair on its back on a rather high bench. Ideal height for average housewife is family ironing board, covered with newspapers, placed before window with good light. Top of chair is left of board; with back splat so high up, it is easy to concentrate on fine bronze powder shadings. Best work in shading, brushwork or striping is done with a certain relaxation conducive to concentration.

Putting on the Freehand "Pillow" Decoration

12. All of the early Hitchcocks had the conventional brushwork on the "pillow" or the "bolster" backs done with a sable brush freehand. If with gold leaf, it was done with varnish size; sometimes with bronze mixed with varnish, as for the rings. See illustration on page 42 for various pillow designs. If you use gold leaf see Chapter VII on the laying of gold leaf. Sometimes the front roll was done similarly in gold leaf. Also on the early chairs, broad lines in gold leaf with a conventional design at the top were used. See illustrations on page 40. You will need a No. 1 round square-pointed sable brush for this.

Cleaning Up the Stenciled Area

13. The next day, after your stenciled area is thoroughly dry, the stenciled parts should be washed with an ordinary face cloth and cold water, sometimes slightly soaped with Ivory soap. Wipe dry immediately with soft clean cloth. This removes all excess powder and leaves the edges sharp and clear. If any powder has accidentally stuck to the varnish, carefully remove this with a small piece of steel wool, No. 00. Varnish over the stenciled areas with furniture varnish. When dry, the chair can be striped. This varnish coat is necessary because with it mistakes can be wiped off readily without injuring the gold stenciling.

LEAF VARIATIONS

Leaf decorations are used traditionally as a design in combination with fruit or flowers in your groupings and many-unit stencils. On page 36 are interesting early and later period leaf designs, one-part and two-part stencils.

No. 1. Small early leaf: one-piece outline cut stencil, shaded as indicated with a curved piece of cut-out linen.

No. 2. Two-unit stencil outline of oak leaf, one unit all veins; another unit cut from separate piece of linen.

No. 3. Two-unit deep gold stenciled leaf. Outline one unit. Midrib and turned-over point, another unit on separate sheet. Veins are fine hairline brushwork.

No. 4. Outline of leaf, one unit. Veins and curved shading cut on separate piece.

No. 5. Maple leaf outline one unit, all veins cut on separate piece.

No. 6. Early grape leaf two-part stencil with lower turned-up section cut separately. Both are shaded with curved cut section of piece of linen.

1

2

3

4

5

6

7

8

9

10

11

12

38

CHAPTER VI

Few things are impossible to diligence and skill.

SAMUEL JOHNSON

STRIPING CHAIRS AND OTHER FURNITURE

Striping was an old trade in itself. In the chair factories one or two men did all the striping with exact proficiency and the speed of lightning. George Lord is said to have striped one hundred chairs a day with the old King's Yellow; these at three cents a chair netted three dollars, a large sum for those days.

Striping Should Be Done with the Whole Arm Motion

1. Striping, often the bugaboo of the beginner, is really one of the simplest and easiest of the decorating processes, certainly needing no head work, but a steady hand only. Like Spencerian writing it should be done with *the whole arm* from the shoulder down in one grand sweep, mostly pulled towards the body. Never try to do any length of line with the fingers and forearm only.

The Third and Little Fingers Guide the Hand

2. On striping, from the *Scientific American* of October 9, 1845: "Long camel-hair pencils (brushes) were used, the artist guides his hand by placing some one of his fingers in such a position that it bears on the edge of the panels, or frame, sliding along as the hand moves with the pencils."

That is just it! The brush, made as described on page 8, is gripped tightly with the thumb and forefinger, and the little finger is the guide that slides down the side post or along the back panel. If pulled along at a good pace, the stripe is bound to be straight, with practice.

Brushes Used in Striping

3. Today it is easy to buy any width of quill striping brush from the heavy ½ inch sign painter's flat striper of camel's-hair, hairs about three inches long, to the finer quill stripers, hairs made of squirrels' tails, about 1½ inches long. But for

fine striping on Hitchcock chairs, Sheraton Fancies, Boston rockers, etc., we must make our own brushes or pencils.

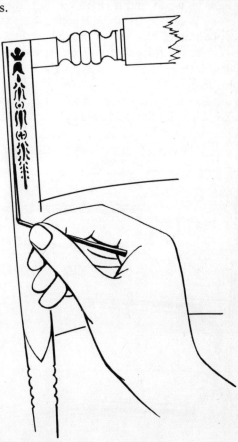

HAND POSITION FOR STRIPING

Making the Hairline Striper

4. Buy two or three ordinary penholders, cut in about half lengths, sharpen the pointed end to a fairly fine point. This makes an ideal large size grip, and when the few hairs are tied to it, it makes a fine stripe. Buy a 1½ inch long No. 4 quill striper from an art store (squirrel's-hair). With a razor blade cut about 25 hairs at the exact base

from this. The hairs at the base should be cut about as round as a darning needle. Tie them onto the pointed penholder with heavy black thread, wound round and round the penholder tightly so that the individual hairs will not pull out. Tie in a double knot and cut with a razor blade very close to knot. Pull out any short hairs, leaving all *uniform length.* Cut off the end slightly, with scissors, so they will all be of uniform length. This is very important.

Preparation of Paint for Striping

5. Obtain a tube of chrome yellow medium ground in japan and a small bottle of japan drier (brown liquid). In an old coffee can top put a teaspoonful of the yellow mixed with the japan drier, add ½ teaspoonful of burnt Sienna (in oil) and a dash of chrome green to the consistency of light cream. To this add a few drops of varnish and mix thoroughly with the ½ inch camel's-hair brush used for the gold rings.

Never use turpentine in striping mixture. It is too likely to spread the stripe. We have observed that many a beginner's work is spoiled, even if the stenciling is very neat and good, by a bright yellow too-wide stripe that fairly hits you in the eye. To get the antique look on Hitchcocks, Boston rockers, bureaus, etc., the whole should *blend* in as a unit, and not have the stripe "kill" the stencil. To gain this effect in your striping, put a dash of burnt Sienna, and a dash of chrome green thoroughly mixed with the yellow. The red neutralizes the green and vice versa, and you have a subdued old yellow. Also, the paint may appear all right in the can cover, but when drawn down the black or brown chair it seems twice as bright. By all means, tone it down to some unity. If you do not want so much bother, use gamboge (in oil) not obtainable in japan. Thin with the drier (not too thin) and this gives an antique old yellow. It is a matter of artistic choice, but our advice is *never* to take any raw yellow out of a tube and stripe with it.

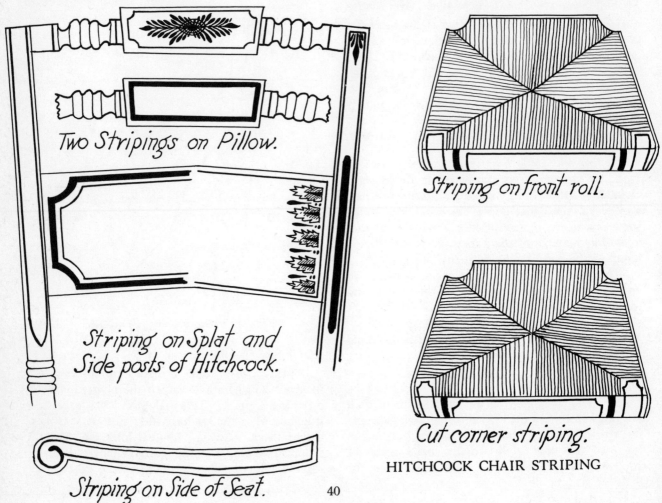

Two Stripings on Pillow.

Striping on Splat and Side posts of Hitchcock.

Striping on Side of Seat.

Striping on front roll.

Cut corner striping.

HITCHCOCK CHAIR STRIPING

40

The Striping Technique

6. Lay the entire striping brush in the yellow paint and smooth it out on a piece of glass; place the point of the brush at top of side upright on Hitchcock chair, pull rapidly down left side of upright to bottom, forming half a point. Make short line across upright top starting with tip of brush. Exactly where this leaves off, with brush reloaded, draw right-hand stripe connecting in point at bottom with left stripe. Stripe other upright and rest of chair. See drawing on page 40.

Striping Circles and Quarter Rounds

7. On pillow the quarter round in each corner is made by swinging the point of striping brush around in an arc. In fact, you can draw a complete circle with the brush well loaded with paint if the tip is used first, gradually letting about ¼ of the brush come on the surface finally. Put round yellow rings on rungs and legs.

Uniform Thickness of Line

8. Good striping must have *uniform thickness* of line its entire length. A straight line drawn in conté crayon on furniture will help the beginner, painting right over it. Where two stripes join at right angles they must join exactly at end of each stripe. If not enough paint is on brush to complete the line, dip in paint, then on glass. To load it right, put point a little way back of where you left off, bear down lightly and continue to desired end. This will all be mastered in time with a little practice.

Where you have a wide gold stripe made with an entire quill, it is usually more interesting to put a yellow hairline about ¼ inch inside gold stripe. It must be entirely parallel to be effective. If there has been any slight deviation in the gold line it is quite simple and effective to put a yellow hairline on one side of the gold line, always on inside of gold line. It gives a finished look.

Striping with Gold Powders and Gold-Leaf Striping

9. There are several methods of applying gold stripes around splats of Hitchcocks, top boards of Sheratons, on bureaus, settees and other furniture where this is required to act as a frame for the stenciling or gold-leaf work.

First Method

1. Dip required size (1½ inch long) squirrel-hair quill in varnish slightly thinned with japan drier. Apply the varnished stripe on the panel, thoroughly rubbed down flat with 00 steel wool. When tacky (similar to stencil tackiness), dip a large wool *bob* in desired shade of bronze powder and rub lightly and evenly right over varnished stripe longitudinally. This will give a uniform, even surface, satiny stripe. When thoroughly dry, wash off with damp cloth all excess powder and varnish the whole panel.

Second Method

2. Mix a normal amount of varnish thinned with japan drier with the desired shade of bronze powder to a heavy cream consistency. Have the desired quill striper thoroughly soaked in this mixture, draw several times across a piece of glass and then apply the stripe where needed. Be careful with the square-pointed quill to have all right angle stripe intersections *very square* on the corners. This is the general method on all long striping like bureaus and settees. Powder used is No. 65 (Both) or No. 60 Coach Striping No. 1 (Venus).

Third Method

3. On shorter lines, up to ten inches, as for chair backs and boxes where line is always straight, it was an old practice to cut the desired width of line out of paper (now tracing cloth). Varnish furniture surface and when the right tackiness for stenciling, apply cut-out line where desired by rubbing the powder with large *bob* longitudinally along the length of cut-out stencil. Hold stencil taut with free hand for a straight line. Where right angle stripes intersect, some care is needed with the cut-out to have the corners sharp and clear. This is the easiest method to get a uniform stripe in widths considerably wider than the hairline yellow stripe.

Fourth Method

4. In gold-leaf striping, much used by old craftsmen, you could then buy gold leaf in about two-inch rolls of varying widths unobtainable today. The roll was simply unrolled along the varnished line made by different width quills. The procedure is the same as for rubbing powder over the varnished stripe, except little wider strips than the line are cut out of a sheet of transfer gold leaf. These strips are applied slightly overlapping along length of varnished stripe until the panel is surrounded. The varnish should be somewhat drier than for stencil tackiness.

Rub a small pad of cotton on back of a sheet of transfer gold leaf; see next chapter. The gold comes off the tissue and remains with uniform brilliance on the varnish line. Do not touch until next day, when excess gold is wiped off with cotton cloth with no pressure.

6

4

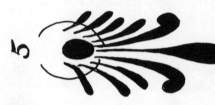

5

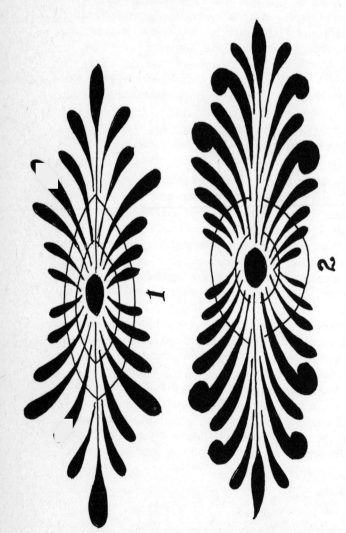

1

2

3

DECORATIONS FOR HITCHCOCK CHAIRS IN GOLD LEAF
1, 2, 3   Common type pillow designs
4, 5   Top of stiles
6   Etched gold leaf

42

CHAPTER VII

*Knowledge is of two kinds: we know a subject ourselves,
or we know where we can find information upon it.*

SAMUEL JOHNSON

GOLD LEAF—ITS USE AND APPLICATION

The early gold-leaf work was used first as a cheaper substitute for the expensive Oriental raised design on Chinese lacquer. Very elaborate gold-leaf trays were decorated in England prior to 1800. In America, trays were beautifully decorated with gold-leaf scroll borders and centers from 1800 to well into the Victorian era.

1. Gold leaf was used only on the finer type of chairs. On the better type of Hitchcock chair, the top pillow or the bolster top often had a brush-work conventional design in gold leaf, see page 40. Sometimes the stiles or side posts, especially on the early chairs (see page 42, stile designs, and often the front roll of the best Hitchcocks, were done with gold-leaf brushwork. See illustration, page 67.

2. Gold leaf was used almost entirely on the Sheraton Fancy chairs, even for the gilt turnings, and always the Chinese-influence Sheratons with the balls between the cross stretchers were gilded with real gold.

3. Many of the "combback" Boston rockers had their rounded top panel corners of gold leaf, with elaborate minute black brush strokes alone or combined with fine etched lines. See illustration, page 59.

4. Gold-leaf scrollwork was used extensively on all types of "bedroom" chairs well into the Victorian era, see modified form, page 132.

5. On some of the less expensive chairs silver leaf was widely used in place of the more costly gold leaf. The old artisans were very clever with this silver leaf, for when they applied two or three coats of thinned orange shellac over the silver only an expert could tell it from the more expensive lemon gold.

Silver leaf does not have any present-day popularity.

Gold Leaf

6. Gold leaf comes in two forms: (a) the loose leaves, 24 in a book, between very thin sheets of orange tissue paper; (b) the transfer gold leaf, which is the *only one the beginner should use*, where the gold is attached to a thin white tissue and is thus very easy to handle. With this transfer gold, the tissue is merely laid down on the sized surface of the design and comes away from the tissue onto the size with no fuss or bother. The gold on tissue can be cut readily into small pieces with scissors for more economy. This transfer gold, while formerly much less expensive, is now $1.35 to $1.50 per book of 24 leaves.

Handling of Transfer Gold Leaf

Note: as transfer gold is attached to a piece of tissue larger than the gold leaf itself — that is, it has an overlap — care must be exercised in placing on your tacky furniture surface only the gold. If in error you put down a border of the tissue, it may stick annoyingly to the furniture where varnished.

Transferring the Design

Trace the design for the pillow back freehand decoration for your Hitchcock from page 42, designs 1, 2, or 3, on a piece of thin tracing paper. On the back of this tracing rub lithopone powder with a cotton wad rubbed into the paper. If you prefer, a piece of white chalk can be rubbed on the back where the design appears and wiped off with a cloth, leaving no excess. Place the chalk side on the pillow back with the design exactly in the measured center of the pillow. With a pencil go over the design carefully, outline each brush stroke. With more practice, this can be put on quickly, all freehand.

GOLD-LEAF MOTIF FOR STILES. FINE LINES ETCHED

RIGHT-HAND CORNUCOPIA AND CENTER CIRCLE MOTIF

DESIGN FOR BOLSTER. GOLD LEAF WITH ETCHED-ON LINES

STENCILS FOR HORN-OF-PLENTY HITCHCOCK CHAIR

44

ONE-UNIT CUT-OUT STENCIL ON UPPER FRONT OF COMMODE. See Work Pattern 13

45

CORNER DESIGN. OPPOSITE CORNER TURNED OVER

TOP SPLAT, CENTER, OF THREE-SECTION DESIGN

FRONT OF SEAT DESIGN

ETCHED GOLD-LEAF DESIGNS FOR SHERATON FANCY CHAIRS
WITH SUPERIMPOSED SHADINGS IN BURNT AND RAW SIENNA

Gold Size

There are various and sundry gold sizes on the market. These are almost essential for fine tray work, but for chair decoration we find that the *thinned varnish used for the stencil* is satisfactory, provided it is quite thin. A good varnish size is made by mixing a furniture varnish with a small amount of turpentine. It must not be thin enough to run even slightly. Use a No. 2 square-end red sable show-card brush. Dip it into the thin varnish, rolling it around to point it up. All fine brushwork is done with *finger motion only*, arm remaining stationary.

Sizes Used in Gold-Leaf Work

The terms SIZE or SIZING are used to describe adhesives by which gold and other leaves are applied to various surfaces.

Gold Size on Hitchcock Pillow Back

Rest little finger on pillow and fill in central oval with varnish. See illustration, Fig. 1, 2, or 3, page 42. With the brush nicely pointed with varnish, and with the thinnest of hairlines, draw the fine long lines either side of the center of oval, spreading the brush at each end and graduating it to a fine point at either side. Next draw fine hairline larger oval around central oval. Starting at the top of graduated brush strokes pull pointed brush down to center oval on each section. Do left-hand upper section next, pulling brush downward toward you with each stroke. Turn the chair slightly and do right bottom and left bottom of conventional design.

If pillow has been rubbed with steel wool No. 00, the varnished design will show up well on the flat surface. If chair is shiny, a little chrome yellow added to varnish will show up on a glossy surface. It is important that lines have sharp non-ragged edges. This is accomplished by having the varnish size neither too thin nor too thick.

Laying the Gold Leaf

The varnish should be almost dry before laying the gold leaf, drier than for the shaded stencil.

Lay the gold side of the transfer leaf down on the "tacky" pattern, *being careful not to lay any of the tissue down on the size*, as it will adhere and you cannot lay more leaf where any part has adhered tissue.

With one hand press a small cotton wad evenly over the tissue backing the leaf, holding the tissue

THREE STEPS IN APPLYING GOLD LEAF

CHALK OUTLINE OF PATTERN ON CHAIR

OUTLINE SIZED IN WITH VARNISH OR GOLD SIZE

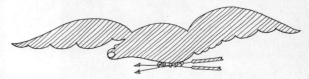

GOLD LEAF LAID ON READY FOR ETCHING

down firmly with the other hand. Lift the tissue quickly; the gold has adhered only to the size where the design is placed.

If the design is not all covered use another leaf, until all varnished areas have the gold attached to the design.

Wait several hours, or a whole day, if you can; then, with a soft piece of cotton, wipe off any excess gold, being very careful not to rub hard, as the thin gold mars very readily and the brilliant effect can easily be spoiled.

The conventional design on the Hitchcock pillow needs no etching and can be varnished with clear varnish next day when thoroughly dry to protect it.

Gold-Leaf Brushwork. Overlay and Etching

On the Boston rocker corner motif, page 63, and also on the Eagle Hitchcock chair, page 71, the gold has superimposed black fine brushwork *together* with etching. Not only is the gold etched, but shading with raw and burnt umber is also used, as is also the case with the gold-leaf eagle, page 113. We will take the example of black line brushwork used together with etching first on the Boston rocker corner motif, page 63.

Trace the larger black lines of the gold-leaf Boston rocker corner on thin tracing paper with

RUNNING BORDER, OAK LEAF AND ACORN
Shade leaves with curved piece of linen

STENCILED OAK LEAF BORDER WITH FLOWERS

48

PRACTICE IN SHADING LEAVES AND FRUIT. See page 25

49

a very sharp medium hard pencil. Put white chalk or lithopone powder on the back of the tracing. Turn the tracing over on top of the gold corner, being careful to have the traced gold edges exactly under the traced lines. The white chalk lines will appear on the gold and will not interfere with the black brush strokes you apply where traced on with pencil from tracing paper.

With a very fine flat-pointed red sable brush No. 1 dipped in the japan black from tube thinned to a flowing consistency with liquid japan drier, with two drops of varnish added, draw carefully the circle and the central cross. Always take off any excess paint from brush on a piece of news-paper before starting each brush stroke. It is also wise for the beginner always to varnish over any gold-leaf work and wait a day until dry before doing black brushwork on gold leaf. Where etch-ing is done, it should be done the same day as the gold leaf is laid, as the needle used in etching may chip off the gold in a ragged uneven line. Etching tool is made of a darning needle. After the entire design is etched, wipe off the roughened surface with a piece of soft cotton. Do not varnish the etching until at least twenty-four hours as it must be thoroughly dry.

TIPS FOR THE GOLD-LEAF USER

Preparation of Surface for Gold Leaf Application

The main difficulties for an amateur in applying the leaf over chair panels or on a table top are in:

a. having the surface smooth and even under the gold.

b. preventing the gold from adhering to the surface at any point whatsoever except where the applied sized design appears. This is especially important on intricate scrolls shown in design for Sheraton chairs, page 109.

Before Putting on Gold Leaf

One or two thin coats of orange or white shellac is the ideal surface sealer. It dries rapidly, contains no oil-like varnishes, and seals out any moisture to which the gold leaf very easily adheres.

If you must apply the gold direct on some enameled surface, then try magnesium powder or talcum powder. Some of the early master chair gilders cut a raw potato in half and rubbed this over the surface to be gilded. The potato starch, when dry, leaves a powder film on which the design is applied with the size, after which gold is applied. When very dry, in a day or two, a moist cloth will take off the powder around the design.

50

CHAPTER VIII

When I was a young man, being anxious to distinguish myself,
I was perpetually starting new propositions. But I gave this over;
for I found that generally what was new was false.

SAMUEL JOHNSON

FINISHING THE CHAIR OR PIECE OF FURNITURE

The "antique finish."

Varnish versus shellac as a final finish.

1. Opinion differs on the final coats of shellac or varnish. After reading the other books and pamphlets published on the subject, we expect to be in controversial "hot water" on finishes. Let us analyze the purpose of final coats.

First: they preserve your handiwork, assuming primarily it is well worthy of careful preservation.

Secondly: they give the old look. Nobody wants an antique or reproduction to shine with varnish like a bright new toy.

Spar Varnish??

If we were a beginner, nothing would discourage us so much at the start as to be told to put on five or six coats of "spar" varnish on a chair we thought practically done, and to rub it down with pumice and oil for hours. To a beginner, and to the author, it does not make much sense.

Old Masters Used Shellac

What has most impressed us in restoring, "touching up," doing over entirely and examining so many thousands of chairs over the years, is the fine condition they presented after a hundred or more years of oxidation and chemical change of the finish. Some of them seemed to have been done last week, yet the stenciling and gold rings were very old. Moreover, countless coats of varnish were *not* used on them originally. This is readily proved when these old chairs are carefully cleaned with soft cloths dipped in "Quakersol," a denatured solvent, to remove dirt. At the same time, it reveals the under layer of decoration. What was discovered? That all early finish coats were *thin shellac*, and sometimes applied not so thinly. This, we would say, held true for about eighty per cent of *all* old finishes.

2. Thin shellac was applied in the old days even over colored finishes as yellow and a beautiful pale blue-green.

A few years ago we restored a beautifully hand-painted bedroom set with exquisitely painted roses and scrolls. The decorations were entirely intact. The finish, however, had accumulated considerable grime and the paint was entirely worn off in places. Luckily the pieces had been finished originally with two very thin coats of orange shellac. This we very carefully washed off from all the pieces with "Quakersol," leaving the lovely blue-green tint intact. All worn places were repainted with an exactly matching flat paint.

Our point is this: if the paint had been covered with two coats of what corresponds to our modern spar varnish, this varnish with age would have oxidized to a dirty olive color. Thus it would have been impossible to remove it without injuring the colorful decorations, and the pieces could not have been restored to their original beauty. It is very fortunate for modern restorers that the old artisans did use *shellac exclusively*. The above process has also been used extensively on yellow pieces, and was eminently successful on the old tan-colored bureau pictured on frontispiece.

3. Varnish is recommended for trays and coffee table tops. There is no question in this modern age, when liquids may eventually ruin your designs, that any and all trays and coffee tables need several coats of the best spar or bar varnish. But it is very unlikely that a wet towel will be draped over the back of your choicely decorated chair; even so, it would not ruin it. Therefore we insist that the easiest and most authentic method today to obtain that antique soft glow and *depth* of transparent luster is with *coats of thin orange shellac*, as in the old method, irrespective of what is printed in the books. Two coats of semi-flat or satin finish varnish will give a similar effect without the rubbing,

51

but the "feel" of the chair will be quite different.

However, to put coat after coat of spar varnish on your finished decorated piece, finally rubbing with pumice and oil, will inevitably give a hard, brittle modern plastic look to your fine old chair no matter how much you rub with pumice. If you feel you must use varnish, use a furniture varnish, *never heavy spar*, and use two coats, rubbing the last only.

4. Fine cabinetmakers never had a quart of *varnish* in their shops. Just for your own satisfaction go to an antique cabinetmaker who restores priceless antiques, where the finish is all-important. Ask him what he uses on his fine pieces, worth hundreds of dollars. His answer will be: successive coats of thin orange shellac — the best made only — sandpapered with finest sandpaper and 00 steel wool *between* the coats. Then it is rubbed with paraffine or linseed oil with a few drops of turpentine added, by dipping a piece of burlap in the best Italian pumice stone with the oil and turps. When he is finished, the piece has that soft satin glow approaching or equaling the old patina you find on the pieces so carefully preserved in the museums. He will tell you, if he is not too secretive, that the final shellac coat or coats are "ragged" on (with a lintless cloth pad) which applies the thin shellac more evenly than can be done with any brush.

5. Shellac finishing is centuries old. Some interesting facts about shellac, as collected and published by the American Bleached Shellac Manufacturer's Association, Inc., are pertinent here. "Shellac is the product of an insect, the lac bug of India, which converts the sap of trees into the shellac of commerce. No other known resin or chemical compound duplicates its qualities. Orange flake shellac gum, cut in alcohol, makes the pure orange shellac in commercial form. Pure shellac is the lac-quer of the ancient artisans. It has been in use for ages. It is natural that the great violin maker would develop his own secrets of shellac application; or that the men who floored the Salle des Glaces at Versailles should have worked out their own technique for using shellac to make those inlaid floors beautiful for centuries. Even the intelligent amateur can get uniformly good results with pure shellac. Seventy per cent of the floors in large cities are being finished with shellac, twenty per cent with sealer, ten per cent with varnish."

PROCEDURE

Finishing Chair with Shellac

6. You have your chair stenciled, striped and the gold rings applied. The next day, when thoroughly dry, the final finishing coats are started. To one quart of the best grade orange shellac (five pound cut — meaning five pounds of dry flake shellac to one gallon of denatured alcohol as a solvent), add one pint of wood alcohol or "Quakersol." Mix with your short flat chiselled brush thoroughly in a larger can. The brush for shellacking is a two-inch chiselled fitch brush or ox-hair with short bristles. This brush should be used for shellacking only and washed out with alcohol and put away dry when not in use.

Method of Applying Shellac

7. Shellac, unlike varnish, dries rapidly and requires no crosswise tip of brush smoothing up. As in painting a chair, the important point in shellacking is to put on an even coat, methodically and part by part, with not too much or too heavy overlapping. Overlaps will show up much more with shellac than with paint. This is why on large areas like bureaus, tables, etc., the final coat is ragged on, dipping the lintless flat cloth pad in the very thin shellac and with long stroke whole arm motion, rapidly smoothing it on without any perceptible overlap. But this is not necessary for a chair.

Methodical Part-by-Part Shellacking

8. Have the back of the chair facing you. Shellac the back of each front leg, working the brush around the leg and turnings. Turn the chair half round, then all around to facilitate shellacking the front and farther side of the legs. Next do the front turned stretcher all around. The back of stiles or side posts come next, brushing up and down one side, then the front, then the other side of the side post. The back splat panel, back of top pillow turning, and front of top pillow or bolster, and front of stenciled panel come next. Turn the chair *around you* to facilitate this. Be careful to get the shellac on the thin top of the stenciled back panel. This also applies to the slightly thicker rounded top of the Boston rocker top panel. Next shellac the side pieces around the seat and the front roll, and lastly the thin round stretchers between the front legs and back stiles.

Air Bubbles Seldom Appear Unless Shellac Is Too Thin

9. If any minute air bubbles occur they can be taken out by brushing back and forth lightly. The main point in shellacking is to work rapidly enough on each section as outlined so there will be no noticeable overlapping.

WORK PATTERN SECTION

WORK PATTERNS

CHAPTER IX

In this chapter we roll up sleeves and go to work as decorators. Here is presented a rich variety of practical projects for the decoration of many pieces of furniture. Care has been taken to present step by step every detail that transforms a plain piece of furniture into a work of decorative art. These lessons are shop-tested, the distillation of over a score of years of professional furniture decoration. In most cases patterns are given in actual size. You need only trace them from the book. Once you get the "feel" of furniture decoration, there is an infinite number of possible variations for original and creative effort.

The following twenty Work Patterns, complete with well-detailed and clear photographs and drawings, will be of considerable help to the amateur decorator. It will enable the beginner to take up his brush and start at once to try out the technical steps explained in the preceding chapters on graining, gold-leaf application, gold rings applied, old and restored stenciling, as well as the actual striping as it appears on the various pieces.

Most patterns in this book are accurate and *full size*, ready for tracing. If necessary to reduce or enlarge a pattern, it is best done cheaply and quickly at a blueprint (photostat) shop.

For the teacher or professional decorator, the following pattern section will be of equal interest because of the rarity of some of the early stenciled chairs and others with the old original gold-leaf applications seldom seen today.

Sources of Furniture Reproductions

As with all antiques, the genuine pieces of early American furniture are becoming increasingly harder to find. In order to satisfy the demand for Hitchcocks, thumbbacks, settees, Boston rockers, captain's chairs, etc., this type of furniture, patterned on identical lines as the classic originals, is being produced today in several New England factories. A few manufacturers and dealers with reproductions suitable for decorating are listed here:

Woodcraft Shop, Rockland, Maine. Settees, television benches, wood-box bars, etc.

Bostonia Rattan Furniture Co., Boston, Mass. Thumbback chairs and nests of tables.

Pilgrim Furniture Mfg. Co., Boston, Mass. All early American reproductions as pictured in this volume.

Hagerty Co., Cohasset, Mass. Knocked-down ladderbacks, etc.

Everett Spaulding, Georgetown, Mass. Hitchcock and Sheraton chairs, bar chairs, etc.

Maurice Spaulding, Georgetown, Mass. Hitchcock and Sheraton settees, child's and captain's chairs.

Miracle Americana, New York, N. Y. Pennsylvania balloon chairs, tables and Hitchcock chairs.

Tell City Chair Company, Tell City, Ind. Will make, on special order, all styles of unfinished chairs.

These shops turn out finished and unfinished furniture. Mass produced, the finished furniture is painted and decorated with stenciling only. Finished furniture, fairly high in price, is distributed by department stores and home furnishing shops. Undecorated furniture, available in white wood, can be bought at modest prices and decorated at home. This manual is dedicated to the home craftsman working on furniture of this type.

Some firms are now offering inexpensive early American furniture in a package, that is, knocked down and ready to set up at home. The Cohasset ladderback chair is such an example. We wish to point out that your approach to decorating is essentially the same, whether it is a Boston rocker fresh from the factory in white wood, or a Boston rocker with a history, stripped of its old finish, down to the bare wood. Either chair can be brought to life by following the step-by-step instructions given throughout this book.

YELLOW THUMBBACK CHAIR

YELLOW THUMBBACK CHAIR
Sometimes Called "Rabbitear Chair"

ABOUT 1830

Yellow painted furniture was next in popularity to the red and black rosewood graining, especially in New England. Not only were thumbbacks done in this old pale yellow like the illustration of a chair on page 55, found in a New Hampshire attic, but also Salem rockers, washstands, one drawer and two deck dressing stands and more elaborate Sheraton Fancy chairs. They were stenciled or ornamented with gold leaf as early as 1800.

This chair, an easy one to decorate since the cut stencil is simple, is placed here as your first decorating project, complete with patterns and instructions.

PREPARATION

Take off all the old rough paint and varnish from an old thumbback which you may have "picked up," see Chapter III, page 11, and sand down thoroughly to original wood with No. 0 sandpaper. Or start to work on an unpainted reproduction.

Decoration and Painting Process

1. Paint chair with two coats of antique yellow, which gives the effect of the old pale yellow with its original thin coat of orange shellac as outlined, Chapter II, page 9.

2. Cut a piece of good quality tracing paper, size of the back panel of your chair. Cut another piece the size of a side post to trace the striping.

3. Trace carefully the entire pattern on page 57, each detail of veining and freehand "Spencerian" scrolls. This is your master tracing for the entire work. *Do not trace hatched lines* on leaves to indicate green brush strokes.

4. With a soft No. 3B pencil blacken up the back of the traced design, wiping off any excess with a soft Kleenex.

5. Turn the tracing over with blacked back and fasten with Scotch tape to the back panel. Scotch tape will not hurt the unfinished surface. Trace off the *outline* only of the stenciled fruit marked A, B, C, D, E, F, and the outline only of the green leaves and brush strokes marked G and H. Also trace the cut corner striping.

6. Paint in with the thin black japan paint, with a No. 2 flat-end, round red sable brush, areas A to F. Be careful to have the black laid on smoothly, otherwise any ridges will show up in the stenciling. Let this black dry thoroughly until next day.

7. While the black is drying, cut out stencil units A, B, C, D, E, F from architect's linen (tracing cloth) as outlined in Chapter IV.

8. Time can be saved while the black is drying on the back panel if next you stripe the chair. Use the same black, only slightly thicker. Put a little more japan black from the tube in a can cover; add *a few drops of japan drier liquid and three drops of furniture varnish.* Mix thoroughly with the No. 2 sable brush.

After you have traced the striping on the side posts and the little conventional motif at the top of the "thumbs," paint in these brush strokes, starting at the *bottom* of the brush stroke, pulling the brush toward you, easing up on the pressure until it ends up in a fine hairline. It is better to practice this stroke on a piece of white cardboard first before doing the top of the posts, as the black paint is hard to remove from the yellow chair if a mistake is made.

After you have these posts carefully done, stripe the chair as shown in the picture, as taken up in detail in Chapter VI on striping. The back panel can also be striped last if you are careful not to smudge the black painted stencil background. Set the chair in a warm dry place, and let it dry thoroughly until next day.

Stenciling on Top of Painted-In Black Designs

1. After a 24-hour period, for safe drying, varnish with fairly thin furniture varnish the entire back panel, being careful to lay it on evenly and uniformly.

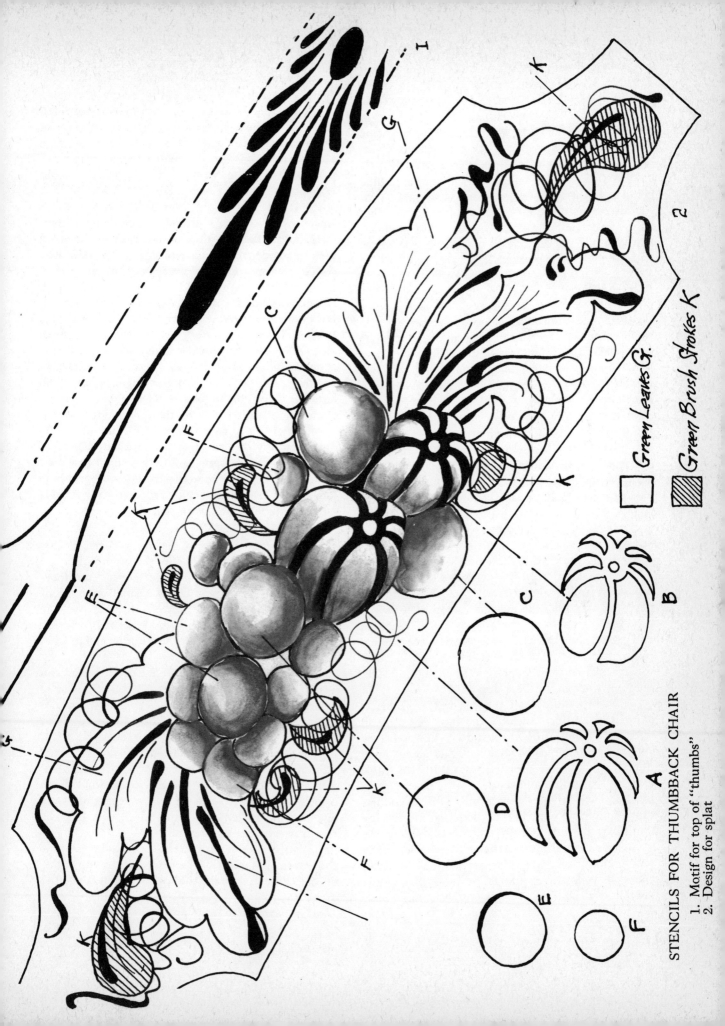

STENCILS FOR THUMBBACK CHAIR

1. Motif for top of "thumbs"
2. Design for splat

Green Leaks G.

Green Brush Strokes K

2. On top panel lay cut stencil A on the section marked A, after the varnish is just the right tackiness. With a good sized *bob*, starting at the center with circular motion, stencil each unit in sequence A, B, C, D, E, F, and G, using the same cut-out for the same sized black painted-in section.

Fade out the bronze powder No. 65 (Both) pale gold so that one fruit and grape will appear to hide behind another. As the pattern is so simple, all the interest is obtained by this fading away effect only. When all the units are stenciled, you are ready to mix the antique green for the side leaves and brush strokes marked K.

Semi-Transparent Olive Green

3. Put about a teaspoonful of japan color chrome yellow medium in a can cover with a smaller amount of Prussian blue (in oil) from your tube. Add a sufficient amount of raw umber, plus small amount of burnt Sienna, to give a soft, not too dark olive green. Sometimes these leaves were more on the blue-green than the olive, but this chair has a lively light olive green for the leaves. While the varnish is still slightly tacky, paint in the leaves and strokes marked K with the No. 2 red sable brush, twirling the brush on the outside outline sufficiently to get a sharp flowing outline. You now will have to wait until the panel is thoroughly dry before putting in the veins on leaves, and the black "Spencerian" scrolls. You can, however, save time by varnishing the chair with rubbed effect, called satin varnish.

4. Next day the fine line veins and brush strokes on leaves and freehand scrolls are traced on the panel by attaching the master tracing with Scotch tape fitted exactly on the already done stenciling and green leaves by placing an evenly white chalked piece of tracing paper (chalk side down) between the tracing and the panel. With a hard pencil, pointed, trace in all these details.

5. With a fine No. 1 pointed red sable brush paint in the veins on leaves and lines X on brush strokes with an antique mustard yellow (chrome yellow medium plus raw umber plus some japan drier, thin flowing consistency). With the same fine brush outline underside of the leaves with black. Twirl in the black scrolls with a circular arm motion. Your chair is done except for the final coat of flat varnish and, as shown in the photograph on page 55, the mottled shell effect seat graining. It would be as authentic to leave the seat yellow, but the following is the rather complicated method of shell seat graining.

METHODS OF SHELL GRAINING ON SEAT OF YELLOW PAINTED CHAIRS

First Method

1. Into a tin coffee can cover put 2 teaspoons of burnt umber (japan color) and 1 teaspoon of raw umber. Mix into this color ¼ pint furniture varnish with a 1″ brush. When thoroughly incorporated with the varnish, this makes a semi-transparent brown.

2. Paint the yellow chair seat a thin coat of this brown. When still wet, proceed as follows.

3. Dip a flat 1″ camel's-hair brush into a small amount of denatured alcohol poured into another coffee can top. Take off excess alcohol on a newspaper. With long curved brush strokes paint with alcohol the outer curve of the shell. The alcohol is antagonistic to the brown paint, and leaves a beautifully veined effect. Dip brush again in alcohol each time until the pointed scallop shell is completed, about 4″ long. Have the shells in swirling position of slightly varying sizes over the entire seat, leaving about a 1½″ margin all around from the black striping to the larger outer shells.

4. With the square tipped brush dipped in the alcohol, push the brown paint forward evenly all around the 1½″ border, forming small shells all around the edge of the seat. In the photograph on page 55 these small shells are distinctly visible on the otherwise well-worn seat.

Second Method

Used often on early Salem rockers. This method is called putty or vinegar graining.

1. Into an empty coffee can cover, mix thoroughly with a two-inch brush a small amount of burnt umber and half a pint of vinegar. Mix the same amount of raw umber and vinegar in another can top. Paint in the seat in alternating patches of this burnt and raw umber.

2. Make a roll of putty from a fresh pound can (with plenty of oil in the putty) about the size of a large thumb. The putty roll is turned around, rolling on flat contact with the vinegar painted chair seat in a little larger than a semi-circle forming a scallop shell. These shells are repeated adjoining all over the chair seat, leaving an inch and a half border inside the black striping. With a smaller putty roll, a little less than one and one-half inches long, roll around the small shells the entire border inside the black striping. The variation in the size of these center whorls gives the interesting effect. The veined effect is a result of the linseed oil in the putty separating the vinegar glaze.

COMBBACK BOSTON ROCKER
ABOUT 1835

59

ROSEWOOD GRAINED COMBBACK BOSTON ROCKER

ABOUT 1835

On page 59 is a fine example of an old curved-seat Boston rocker with "combback" top panel and gold-leaf etched corners. The arms are early style light mahogany. These chairs, formerly known as Windsor rockers, were once produced in considerable quantity. The combback type is rarer and more desirable than the ordinary round-top Boston rocker. While quite plentiful a few years ago, today they are hard to find. If you have one in good condition without a cracked seat or mended arms, count yourself fortunate!

PREPARATION FOR STENCILING

1. If chair needs gluing or mending of arms at the back, take it to a cabinetmaker.

2. If back panel design is in good condition, by all means trace it off, if only for a record of the original. These designs, no matter how faint or partially obliterated, are increasingly hard to find for Boston rocker top panels.

If your chair is in fair condition, i.e., where the old shellac finish is rough in spots, as on the seat, it will need only thorough sandpapering; first use No. ½ sandpaper and smooth with No. 0 sandpaper. After recording (on traceolene) any existing pattern on the top panel it is better to scrape this panel with your steel scraper or a piece of glass, and then sandpaper very smoothly. The arms, usually mahogany or cherry wood, must always be scraped with a steel scraper or glass and smoothly sandpapered.

If your chair has white enamel paint or very heavy coats of paint applied years ago, this must be removed entirely with paint remover.

3. Paint the chair one or two coats of Venetian red or burnt Sienna (ground in japan), sanding with No. 0 sandpaper between the coats. Grain for the rosewood finish and apply the antique walnut varnish stain as detailed in Chapter III. Oftentimes the old rockers had the top panel design grained, but we prefer the top panel entirely black to show up the stenciling to advantage.

4. On a piece of tracing paper trace the outline of the gold-leaf corner and the heavier internal black lines as a guide for your fine black brushwork. Do not trace the very finely shown etched lines.

5. It is best to trace on the gold-leaf corners and apply the gold leaf *before* stenciling the central motif. Any varnish application, if not entirely hard and dry, may retain specks of flying gold. This is not easy to remove even with a turpentine moistened cloth.

Rub the panel down to a flat finish with No. 00 steel wool. Trace on the left corner motif by placing a chalked or lithopone powder treated piece of white paper between your tracing and the chair back, chalk side down. *Turn over* the tracing and trace the right-hand corner outline only, as done for the left corner.

6. Apply a thin even coat of furniture varnish or gold size to the entire outlined sections, right and left motif, where the gold leaf is to be laid on with a No. 2 flat end red sable brush. When almost dry, lay the transfer gold leaf face down on the slightly tacky varnish, as explained in Chapter VII, page 47. Continue with sections of gold leaf until both corners are entirely covered with the gold.

Wait about three hours until the applied gold leaf has dried properly, but not too hard for etching.

7. Wipe all surplus gold from the corners with a pad of cotton. Copy black detailed lines on tracing. Place this over the left corner and with a chalked piece of paper between the tracing and gold corner (chalk next to gold) trace on all heavy lines. This will leave chalked white lines superimposed on the gold leaf.

Turn over tracing and trace similarly on the right gold corner.

These lines (showing up white on the gold) are painted in with thin japan black, using No. 1 finest pointed sable brush. The heavier lines may be

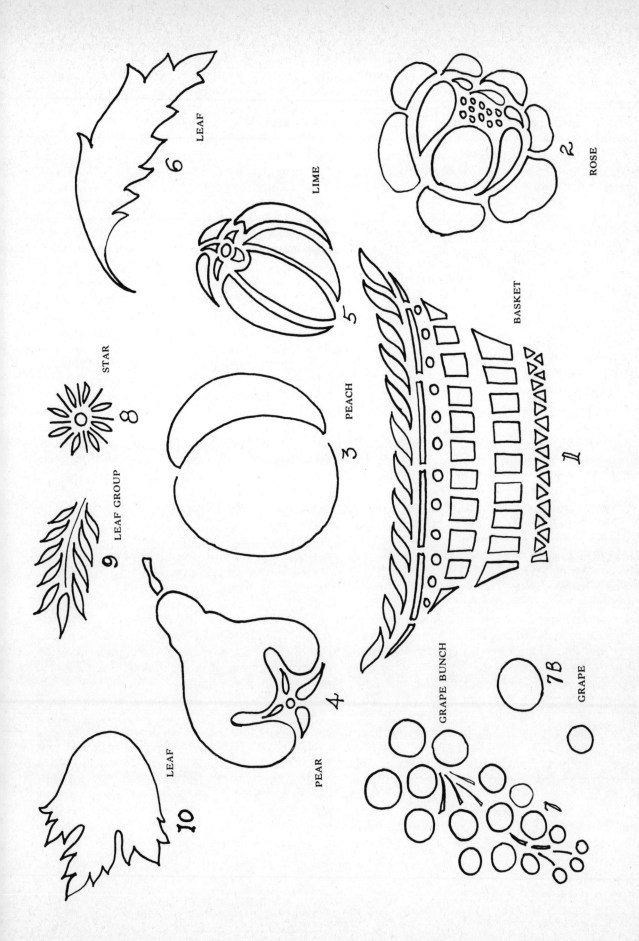

6 LEAF

2 ROSE

5 LIME

3 PEACH

8 STAR

9 LEAF GROUP

BASKET

1

4 PEAR

GRAPE BUNCH

7B

GRAPE

10 LEAF

CENTER STENCIL FOR BACK PANEL OF CHAIR

61

etched in with a blunt pointed knitting needle. A finer etching may be done with an ordinary sewing needle. After both corners are entirely etched, wipe them over with a dry soft cloth. The back panel must wait until these corners are very dry and hard next day before you varnish entire panel for stenciling.

8. Next step, to save time while these are drying, is to put on the ¼ inch gold border around the center panel. This may be done by either of two methods.

First Method

With a No. 4 short quill striper, see page 8, draw the lines carefully with the clear furniture varnish. When about the tackiness for stenciling, dip a wool or velvet pad in a gold bronze, matching as nearly as possible the color of the gold corners. With the pad heavily loaded, wipe it along the varnished line evenly. In about two hours this border line is then wiped over with a damp cloth to remove excess gold powder.

Second Method

Mix matching corner gold powder with furniture varnish to a thick cream consistency, thin slightly with japan drier, and with the No. 4 short quill striper well loaded with gold paint, draw in the border. Have all corners sharp and squared nicely.

9. While waiting for the back panel to dry, put on the gold rings as shown in the photograph, page 59. Run the gold paint on the front leg turnings a little back of halfway round.

10. Also to save time, the chair can now be striped in old dull yellow.

The picture on page 59 shows in detail all hairline striping on seat, back panel, legs, the seven back spindles, and two larger uprights. The cut corner and triangle striping on the back panel was widely used and adds interest. Let all this striping dry until the next day.

11. Directly on your architect's linen trace the sketched units Nos. 1–10 shown on page 61. The center of seat cut-out unit is shown on page 63, but the small side motifs on the seat are on page 74.

Cut out of your linen top panel units Nos. 1–10, the front of seat design, and the small side units Nos. 4 and 5.

The next day, before applying your stencil varnish coat on the panel and seat front, measure with pencil point the exact center of each. When the right tackiness, place the exact center of the seat stencil on the center pencil mark and with No. 65 bright gold bronze stencil in uniformly the entire cut-out. Exactly in the center of your guiding yellow hairlines stencil in the two side seat motifs with the same bronze.

12. After applying furniture varnish to entire back panel, when it is the proper tackiness, proceed to stencil as follows:

a. Center the basket cut-out No. 1. With silver powder used heavily in its center, fade to the edges with less powder. Lift the unit and with *bob* dipped in dark gold or copper bronze, rub it lightly *once* over the center.

b. Stencil the rose unit No. 2 each side of basket, small dots in silver, outer edges of petals No. 65 bright gold shading to red bronze (fire) at base of petals. Lift rose cut-out and touch the *bob* lightly once with the red bronze in center of dots.

c. Stencil with No. 65 gold the peach unit No. 3 in the center of basket. Place it down into the basket. Detailed instructions for this peach technique and the pear No. 4 unit to the left are on page 25.

d. Stencil lime unit No. 5 to right of peach, using deep gold faded away sharply towards peach.

Next stencil two leaves unit No. 6 using separate curved piece of linen. First right leaf, wipe linen clean, turn over and stencil left leaf. See photograph, page 59.

The right and left grape bunches unit No. 7 are next put in with deep gold at bottom. Use No. 65 bronze on larger top grapes. Unit No. 7 need not be turned over for right bunch. With unit 7B large circle shade with silver more grapes in blank spaces at top of each bunch. Intersperse small circle 7B at blank spaces towards bottom of each bunch. Shade each separate grape from top fading to bottom of circle cut-out. See detailed grape shading on page 25.

Put in the four silver star-flower units No. 8 as shown in photograph, and the little leaf group No. 9 over the top stars either side.

Lastly, fill in behind your fruit with leaf unit No. 10 with deep gold bronze, no shaded veins needed, but fade the leaf points sharply to black behind the fruit. Your stenciled rocker panel is now complete. Allow this to dry until next day, then wipe all the stenciled areas with a damp cloth to remove excess powder.

13. You are now ready to put the final finishing coats on the entire chair, back panel and arms included. Give the chair two even coats of the best thin orange shellac. See Chapter III. The final coat, when thoroughly hard and dry, should be rubbed carefully with 00 steel wool and then dusted off with tack cloth. If you prefer two coats of satin finish varnish, space them a day apart with no final rubbing.

Your chair now is an authentically reproduced 1835 Rocker and undoubtedly a future heirloom.

GOLD-LEAF CHAIR CORNER ON BACK PANEL
Dark shading with brush, fine shading with needle

STENCIL PATTERN FOR COMBBACK BOSTON ROCKER, FRONT SEAT ROLL. No shading

63

ORIGINAL TWO-SLAT HITCHCOCK TYPE CHAIR
ABOUT 1828

64

TWO-SLAT HITCHCOCK TYPE CHAIR
With Boston Rocker Type Top

ABOUT 1828

This untouched original rosewood grained chair with rush seat is interesting principally for the unusual early decoration, combining shaded gold leaf with cut stencil. The close-up illustration on page 64 shows the detail of shading nicely. The shaded bird is similar to some seen on the better early trays and probably was done by an expert tray decorator.

PROCEDURE

1. After your chair has been properly sanded smooth, paint red; grain in rosewood finish, and apply the antique walnut stain as detailed in Chapter III. Rub down the walnut varnish stain flat, where you are to decorate.

2. From page 66 of actual sized details, trace on tracing cloth the all black snowflake corner motif and the oval design in solid black around the gold-leaf shaded fruit. These two details are the only stenciling.

On a piece of tracing paper trace the gold-leaf fruit design and the gold-leaf side motif to be placed on the two upright side posts. On another piece of tracing paper the size of the bottom splat, trace the bird and leaves in outline only. The gold-leaf stars and conventional motif, shown under the bird design, page 67, are on the front roll of the seat, to be applied in gold leaf. They are not seen in photo.

3. Measure the center, top splat of your similar chair, and with the chalked back of your fruit tracing, in the center of the splat trace the outline of the apple, the leaves and the grapes, with a 4H hard pencil.

Trace on the running ivy design on each side of upright post or stile, being careful to center it exactly on each upright.

Trace on the bird and leaves, centering exactly on the bottom splat by the same chalk-back method.

On the center of the chair's front roll on the seat, center accurately the two stars and scroll conventional motif you have just traced.

4. All the gold-leaf decorations are now on your chair in fine white chalk lines and ready to put on with your gold size or thinned furniture varnish with a No. 2 flat-end red sable brush, or if you prefer, a pointed red sable brush. If the larger area fruit on top panel and the bird and leaves are done first, by the time you have all the units sized in, these larger areas may be the right tackiness to lay on your transfer gold. For details in laying on the gold refer to Chapter VII. When the gold is entirely laid on all the units you can save time while waiting until the next day to do the stenciling by cutting out the snowflake corner motif and the cut-out oval border around the fruit.

Next day carefully wipe off all excess gold with a small pad of cotton or cheesecloth. Varnish the top splat for stenciling and varnish over all your gold-leaf applications. When the top panel is the proper tackiness, stencil each snowflake conventional motif exactly centered above the two side posts. Stencil the oval around the fruit. The gold bronze to use is the nearest match, of the many shades obtainable, to the gold leaf you have applied.

You must now wait until the next day for the shadings on the fruit and the lower splat bird and leaves decoration.

5. Now we shade gold leaf on top and bottom splats. The main feature of this early chair illustrated on page 64 is the very fine shading on the fruit and bird and leaves. This transparent overlay is composed of two shades blended together.

Into a small cover squeeze a quarter tube of transparent gamboge (in oil). To this add a small amount of raw umber. Thin down this color with about a teaspoon of furniture varnish with a few drops of refined linseed oil added. Load a No. 2 red sable brush with this semi-transparent shade,

DESIGN FOR UPRIGHTS, DONE IN GOLD LEAF WITH BLACK BRUSHWORK

DESIGN FOR TOP SPLAT, HITCHCOCK TYPE CHAIR
Fruit group in gold leaf and oil colors

66

CORNER STAR DONE IN NO-SHADE STENCILING,
MATCHING GOLD LEAF

Above. BIRD AND LEAF DESIGN, BOTTOM SPLAT, GOLD LEAF WITH OIL COLORS
Below. RUNNING IVY DESIGN IN GOLD LEAF, FRONT SEAT ROLL, TWO-SLAT HITCHCOCK CHAIR

67

press brush on newspapers and lay on carefully with quick firm brush strokes the lighter sections of the apple, apple leaves and grapes, and the three cherries on the right.

The darker shadings on the apple, leaves and grapes are shaded with a similar transparent overlay composed of burnt Sienna and a little raw umber mixed as you did for the lighter shading. Put sufficient linseed oil with the burnt Sienna mixture so this will not dry too rapidly. Apply the darker shading as seen in photograph, page 64. With a No. 2 round flat-end red sable brush dipped in clear varnish and pressed on newspapers, blend these two transparent colors so there is no perceptible dividing line. The darker shade of the three cherries is shaded with the same burnt Sienna mixture, to which is added a small amount of crimson lake or alizarin for a redder color.

Shade the bird and leaves with the lighter gamboge mixture, making a black dot for the eye. When the grapes and leaves are dry sufficiently, add a dull yellow dot as shown on page 66 on each grape and brush in the veins on apple leaves with thin raw umber, using finest water-color brush.

There is no shading on the front roll gold. The side posts' gold leaves have finest veins done with thinned raw umber. After your shading is finished, you can stripe the chair in antique yellow as shown in the illustration.

Wait two days until all the decorations are thoroughly dry. On succeeding days two coats of orange shellac are applied as detailed in Chapter VIII. The final coat should be rubbed down carefully with No. 00 steel wool, and wiped carefully with a tack cloth. You now have reproduced one of the most unusual chairs we have found, and if properly executed, you have a chair of which you can be justly proud.

Note: if you have a new rush or flag seat in your chair, give it two coats of varnish a day apart. Do not worry if the flags are quite green in color. They will soon dry out to a soft antique light brown color that will blend properly with the rosewood chair.

ALTERNATE DESIGNS FOR ANY HITCHCOCK CHAIR FRONT ROLL

DUNCAN PHYFE TYPE CHAIR, ETCHED GOLD EAGLE

ABOUT 1810–1825

69

DUNCAN PHYFE TYPE CHAIR WITH CANE SEAT

ABOUT 1810–1825

This two-splat chair, pictured on page 69, with etched gold-leaf eagle on top splat and very early style multiple conventional leaf stencil on bottom splat, is exceedingly rare and interesting. Any gold-leaf eagle on an old chair is extremely hard to find today, and particularly one as well preserved as this is over the years. It was undoubtedly done by an expert craftsman.

1. If you have a similar chair, sandpaper carefully and use the brown graining method as outlined in Chapter III, page 15. After the brown antique coat is thoroughly dry, rub down the two splats, side posts and front roll with 00 steel wool to a flat finish.

2. Trace the entire eagle and stencil motif on the lower splat in every detail, omitting only the center vertical motif on the bottom splat, and the small conventional design on the front roll. This tracing of eagle and compound leaf conventional design on bottom splat is done on good quality tracing paper. Center unit is traced directly onto the tracing linen to be cut out as single unit stencils.

3. With a chalked or lithopone paper between eagle tracing and the top chair splat, trace the outline of eagle, claws and arrows with a 4H hard pencil. Be careful to have each wing tip of the eagle an equal distance from the side uprights.

This eagle is all that is in applied gold leaf, except on the old chair, illustrated on page 69, where all the wide striping was in gold leaf. This you can do if at all expert, but it is not necessary as the striping may well be done with a double hairline width striper in clear varnish, and the No. 65 gold bronze powder wiped over when sufficiently tacky with a large woolen *bob*.

4. Fill in white outlined eagle with thin furniture varnish or gold size, applying very smoothly with no brush marks. Use the finest brush you have for the arrows and claws.

5. When the varnish or size is almost dry or more tacky than for stenciling, lay on your transfer gold as detailed in Chapter VII, page 47.

While you are waiting for this to dry hard, cut out the small separate one-piece stencil on the center of the bottom splat, No. 2 right-hand perpendicular motif, and the circle No. 3, and the small conventional design No. 4 for the front roll, which you have already traced on the architect's linen.

For the compounded leaf stencil, which, you will notice on the chair, is not turned over but merely reversed, you will need four distinct units. It is rather difficult to split up this leaf arrangement into units, but we seem to see four distinct cut units.

Units on our pattern are nicely spaced, so that you can trace them directly on one sheet of linen.

Unit 1 is the top and bottom scroll and the long thick vein, and the two spreading veins on the upper and lower leaves nearest the scroll.

Unit 2 is the upper and lower leaves nearest the scroll.

Unit 3 is the next two leaves upper and lower, which you will notice are larger and longer than the first pair of leaves nearest the scroll.

Unit 4 is the large leaf at the end.

6. After you have cut out the four unit stencil pattern, on the lower splat and the front roll conventional design, varnish the lower splat and the front roll with your thinned furniture varnish. When the right tackiness, measure the center of the front roll and stencil the conventional motif with either No. 65 bronze or brushed brass. Measure the exact center of the bottom splat and stencil exactly perpendicular the small up and down conventional design, right-hand part of No. 2. The round center circle is cut out separately, to one side, and is next stenciled in where you have faded the gold away in the center.

You are now ready to do some complicated stenciling. Place unit 1, which is the scrolls, the long vein and the two short curved veins, near the center vertical conventional design, as shown in the rendered sketch on page 71, and stencil in solid with bright No. 65 bronze.

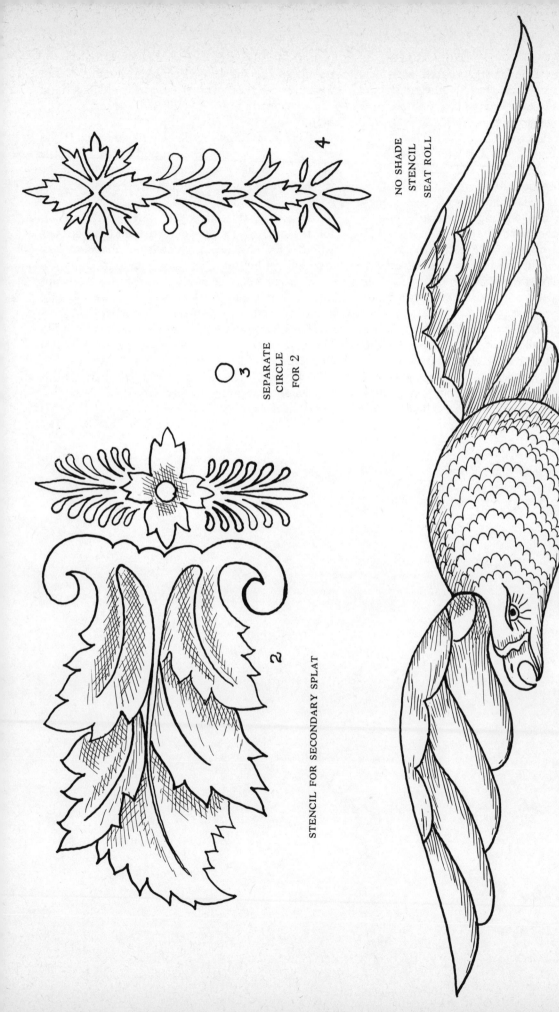

4

SEPARATE
CIRCLE
FOR 2

3

2

STENCIL FOR SECONDARY SPLAT

NO SHADE
STENCIL
SEAT ROLL

1

STENCIL PATTERN, GOLD-LEAF EAGLE, TOP PANEL, DUNCAN PHYFE CHAIR

71

Next take unit 2, and with brushed brass or a deeper gold bronze shade carefully the upper and lower first pair of leaves, leaving it quite dark near the outstanding veins (previously stenciled), with little or no bronze on the *bob*.

Next stencil unit 3, starting with the edges of the upper and lower leaves and fading it away rapidly with no bronze near where the veins will be.

Then stencil in the second pair of veins in these two leaves with No. 65 bright bronze, using on No. 1 unit only the short curved veins.

Lastly, stencil in the large end leaf, fading it away so it appears to be behind the second pair of leaves. You already have the central vein stenciled in from your first scroll unit with heavy midrib. vein.

Your stenciling is now completed. By this time your gold eagle should be sufficiently dry to wipe off the excess gold with a small dry cotton pad.

7. We recommend etching gold leaf when it is not too dry, as it is less likely to chip and spoil the lines of the etching needle. With chalked back tracing of the eagle, trace in all the etching detail with a very sharp pencil over the etching lines. This will make fine white lines all over your gold eagle in chalk.

Take a darning needle or coarse etcher and etch the heavy wing lines and the eye. For the body, the wiggly lines, and the fine etching on the wings, you will need a fine needle, see instructions, page 62, on etching.

Of course, this tracing in with white chalk is for the amateur; only an expert and the artisan who did the old chair accomplished all the etching freehand without an etching guide.

8. The same day you can stripe the chair, and all that is now necessary is to shellac two coats the next day, and rub down the final coat with No. 00 steel wool. If you prefer satin varnish, wait a day between coats and no rubbing is necessary on the final coat.

Your eagle chair, if properly executed, will be a constant joy over the years, and of course will never tarnish.

72

TURTLEBACK, ABOUT 1830
Original multi-unit fruit stencil. Gold leaf on top stile and bolster back top
See page 33 for actual-size shading

OLD TURTLEBACK HITCHCOCK CHAIR
ABOUT 1830

FROM ASHBURNHAM, MASSACHUSETTS, FACTORY. RESTORED DECORATIONS ON PILLOW TOP, STILES AND SEAT FRONT. BACK SPLAT ALL ORIGINAL DESIGN

Remarks

If you have an old turtleback Hitchcock or a modern reproduction, this multiple-fruit splat decoration is an example of good early stenciling. Notice the leaves have *two* early methods of veining, the large central leaf with a curved cut-out and the repeated surrounding grape leaf with cut-out separate vein unit.

PROCEDURE

1. Prepare your chair for decorating in the rosewood grain as detailed on pages 14, 15.

For master tracing, refer to the shadings on units as indicated on page 34.

2. Trace directly on architect's linen the cut-out units Nos. 1 and 1A through 11. Varnish back splat evenly with the thinned furniture varnish. When the proper tackiness, stencil unit 1 and 1A in the upper left-hand turtleleg and the lower right-hand. Wipe clean, turn over and stencil the upper right-hand turtleleg and the lower left-hand.

3. Use your No. 65 (Both) or brushed brass. With unit No. 2 placed as shown on page 75 and with a curved piece of linen, cut out separately, shade in the large central leaf. Next, fruit unit No. 3 is placed on right hand above this leaf; shade as indicated. The two-unit peach seems to hide behind this No. 3 fruit and the tip of large leaf. Shade No. 5 peach unit as indicated, using deep gold near the edge. Place No. 6 peach unit over No. 5 and shade with bright No. 65 gold powder.

No. 4 large lime is now placed left of large leaf so that it seems to rest nicely in the curve of the leaf base.

With No. 8 leaf cut-out, shade in as shown in the sketch, one above the large lime No. 4; one over the No. 3 fruit; one over the peach, Nos. 5 and 6; one to right of the peach and a tip of No. 8 below peach; one under leaf No. 2; then place background leaf No. 8 on the left behind the strawberries as shown.

Stencil small lime unit No. 7 above the leaf and repeat three times the currant bunch No. 9 unit as shown.

Next place the three strawberry units No. 10 in silver powder or No. 65 bright gold. Use No. 11 unit in red or copper bronze to complete the strawberries. The fruit grouping is done. The freehand top of stile unit No. 12 is put on in gold leaf; see page 47 for gold-leaf application. Units No. 4 and 5 are now stenciled on each stile and unit No. 2 is stenciled on the seat front.

4. Around the oval back splat is a $\frac{1}{8}$ inch narrow line of statuary bronze put in with a quill brush. See instructions for lining, page 41.

5. Stripe your chair in a dull yellow hairline stripe, put on the gold rings as shown and when dry, in 24 hours, shellac with two coats of orange shellac or two coats of rubbed effect. Varnish one day apart. If shellac is used, rub down your chair with 00 steel wool.

DESIGN FOR STILES ON TURTLEBACK CHAIR
Also for Front Stretcher of Settee.   Flower fits over cross

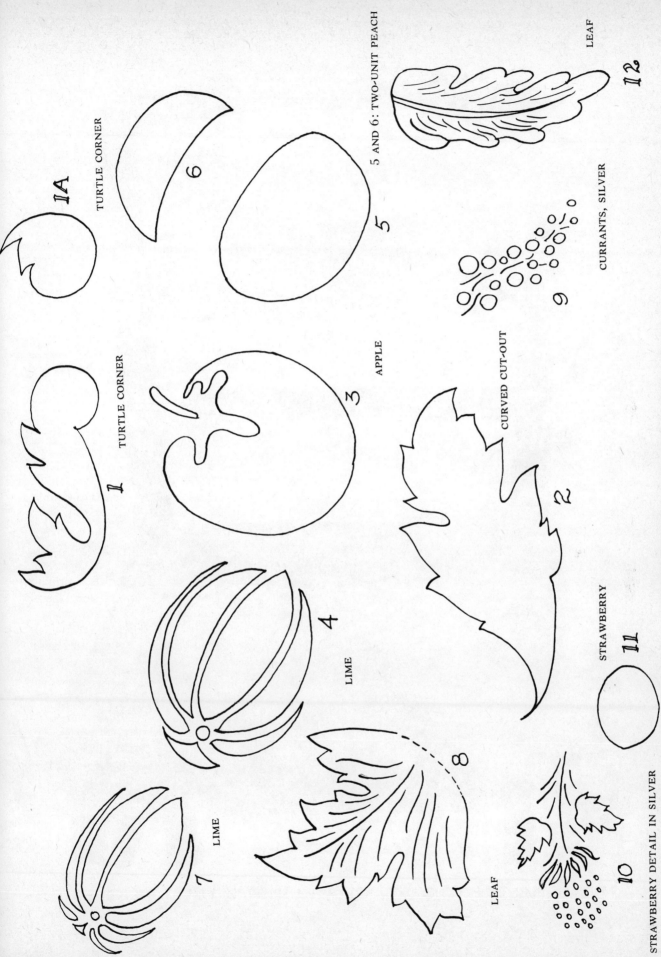

TURTLE CORNER

IIA

TURTLE CORNER

1

6

5

5 AND 6: TWO-UNIT PEACH

3

APPLE

CURRANTS, SILVER

9

LEAF

I2

CURVED CUT-OUT

2

4

LIME

STRAWBERRY

II

7

LIME

8

LEAF

STRAWBERRY DETAIL IN SILVER

I0

STENCIL FOR TURTLEBACK HITCHCOCK

75

HORN-OF-PLENTY HITCHCOCK, RARE WITH SPLAT ENTIRELY STENCILED
ABOUT 1820

CORNUCOPIA-BACK OR HORN-OF-PLENTY CHAIR

ABOUT 1820

This transition chair between the early Sheraton and the more widely distributed wide splat Hitchcock chair is a beautiful example of the very early minute *bob* stenciling on the smaller than usual cut-out cornucopias. In fact, it is the only chair we have seen where the two cornucopias were not the more common etched gold leaf. The top round bolster, the side uprights and the front roll are brushwork gold-leaf applications, as was the usual practice on these beautifully executed chairs.

The chair is *brown* rosewood grain, explained on page 15, done with a brush and wooden comb, and the striping is the finest of hairlines, with the rings in real gold leaf.

You can see by the photograph and as explained on page 3 that here is stenciling with the real gold powder that must have been done with the finest of *bobs*, in the freehand manner, as on the very early metal trays. This finishes for all time, for us at least, the manipulation of the so-called "velvet wrapped finger," so frequently espoused by modern artisans.

PROCEDURE

1. Remove all paint down to the bare wood on a similar cornucopia chair. Sand down carefully and grain in the brown method explained on page 15 and finish ready for decoration with the dark oak varnish stain. See page 16.

2. Paint the face of the cornucopia back splat with two coats of your thin japan black paint, and rub down the entire chair with 00 steel wool before starting to decorate.

3. Trace with a hard pencil the entire back panel drawing, and the top bolster gold-leaf design as well as the gold-leaf side post motifs. The front roll gold-leaf design can be traced from the pattern on page 74. If you want the front roll gold-leaf motif more elaborate, trace one of the Hitchcock seat roll patterns used for stenciling and apply it with the gold-leaf technique.

4. It is merely a matter of choice, but we prefer to put on the gold leaf *before* we do the back splat stenciling so any flying gold will not attach itself to the not entirely dry stenciled surface.

5. With the chalked, or lithopone powder-rubbed back of your gold-leaf tracings, apply the traced side post, top bolster, and front roll designs. Use a very sharp 4H pencil as these chalk tracings must outline very fine and accurate white lines on the flat, rubbed down surfaces of your chair.

6. With the finest flat-tipped red sable brush you have, using your gold size or thinned furniture varnish, apply the gold-leaf size to the chalked patterns on the side posts, bolster back and front roll of your flat rubbed chair. See pages 47, 50 for explicit details.

7. When the size or varnish is almost dry or very slightly tacky, lay on your transfer gold leaf, cut to small sizes that will entirely cover the tacky areas. See gold-leaf applications, page 47.

8. In about three hours wipe off very carefully with a pad of cotton the surplus gold and the adhered gold leaf will be attached to your chair in the exact pattern traced on it.

9. We prefer to etch our gold-leaf motifs on bolster and two side stiles before it is too hard. It is less likely to chip, especially on furniture, under the etching needle. Transfer all the brushwork, but not the fine etched lines, to the bolster back and the stiles, by laying the tracing exactly on the blank gold leaf, and with a sharp pencil go over these fine lines, holding the pattern, without slipping, to the chair with the left hand. The fine chalk lines will show up on your blank attached gold leaf. With a very fine brush and your japan black thinned slightly with the varnish or gold size (not turpentine), brush in this fine detail. When dry, etch in the hairlines as shown in the sketch. Let this dry until next day, when the gold-leaf areas should have a coat of furniture varnish

3

4

7

2

CURVED CUT-OUT STENCIL

8

1

78

STENCIL FOR HORN-OF-PLENTY HITCHCOCK CHAIR

5

BOTTOM OF HORN

9

CURVED CUT-OUT

6

applied, after you have applied the varnish for stenciling the cornucopia back splat. This is to protect against any mistakes in yellow hairline striping, as they are more easily wiped off from a protective varnish coat.

10. Stenciling the back panel. This back panel stenciling is the finest work we have yet observed on any chair back. It can be accomplished only with expert care and the use of the smallest *bobs*. Moreover, it cannot be stenciled all at once the same day, but different areas are stenciled a day apart, or the effect of the sections hiding behind each other or fading into the next unit is lost.

On this chair, original color variation was gained by adroit use of asphaltum shading, a process once popular, but not recommended for beginners.

You have your master tracing of this panel taken from the book.

STENCILING THE TWO CORNUCOPIAS

This complicated and unusual pattern is hard to break up into units. The original was undoubtedly "broken down" into many small units, but to simplify this procedure we have divided it into two main units, Nos. 1 and 2. No. 3 is cut out for the larger circle at the apex of the horn, and circle No. 4 is to be saved when cut out and placed inside circle No. 3 to give a uniform circle about ⅛″ wide around the small flower unit at the horn apex.

PROCEDURE

1. Varnish all black painted right and left cornucopias. While waiting for the varnish to become the right tackiness, cut out all units on page 78, Nos. 1 through 9. See page 21. For cutting small circles with a single edge razor blade, place your cut-out entire unit No. 1 on the varnished right cornucopia so the star with cross in center is exactly centered on the center circle on your chair.

2. The small star at apex of the cornucopia at the right should be exactly centered on the right small apex circle of your cut-out chair splat. Carefully stencil in this entire No. 1 unit as shown on page 78 on the two-toned picture showing every minute and intricate shading. For this use your smallest *quill bob* as shown on page 25.

3. When unit No. 1 is all shaded nicely, place unit No. 2 exactly over what you have already stenciled through No. 1. On both these units the cut-outs No. 8 and No. 9 are used as guides for the small *bob* in shading the large leaf and the melon with minute circles. The two fruits above the large bottom melon are *freehand bob* work and are shaded without any cut-out guide.

4. After using the two-toned illustration for shading No. 2 unit, lift the tracing cloth and place the cut-out No. 3 circle on the cornucopia right-hand apex circle. Place No. 4 unit inside this No. 3 unit and using the *bob*, make the circle around the star flower. Unit No. 5 is at the bottom of cornucopia. Unit No. 6 is placed each side of the wide right-hand cut-out at the base of the small star and four curved line cut-outs. Unit No. 7 is repeated grape unit used five times as indicated in top of cornucopia.

5. After you have stenciled all of the right cornucopia, wipe your linen carefully with a turpentine moistened cloth, wipe dry with another clean cloth and reverse the units and stencil the left cornucopia to match the right-hand one.

6. Next day stripe chair with the finest hair striper, put on the rings as indicated in the photograph, page 76, and after waiting two days give your chair two coats of the best thinned orange shellac. Rub down with 00 steel wool and wipe off carefully with tack cloth.

ANTIQUE YELLOW SALEM ROCKER WITH NATURAL MAHOGANY ARMS
ABOUT 1830

80

YELLOW DECORATED SALEM ROCKER

ABOUT 1830

1. Sand down carefully your Salem rocker, especially the seat and the back panel. If painted with white enamel, clean off entirely with paint remover, see Chapter III, sand down and paint two coats of antique yellow detailed under pattern No. 1. These coats should be spaced a day apart or more, and sandpapered with No. 00 sandpaper between coats.

2. Scrape and sandpaper carefully the arms, which are either solid mahogany or cherry wood. After the last coat of yellow, shellac arms two coats with orange shellac, diluted. When arms are thoroughly dry rub with No. 00 steel wool, a piece of burlap dipped in paraffine or rubbing oil and good Italian pumice stone.

3. On a sheet of architect's linen the size of the book page trace the units Nos. 1-11. Cut these out as detailed in Chapter IV on cutting the stencil.

4. The photograph on page 80 shows clearly the placing of these units. Lay the different cut-out units on the yellow chair panel and with a medium soft pencil trace in the outlines: No. 1 unit in center; No. 2 unit to left, hiding behind slightly; No. 3 unit to right of No. 1; No. 4 unit hanging down slightly over the right of peach; large leaf No. 5 to left of pear No. 2, and to right of peach No. 3; No. 6 bunch of grapes to left, and right of the larger leaves.

Draw in unit 7, single grapes, the larger circle in space above the unit bunch No. 6 and smaller No. 7 circle, amongst the grapes in the bunch (No. 6 unit). For the stars (five of them), we merely draw a small circle the size of No. 7 unit, as shown in the photograph.

This completes what is to be painted in with your thinned japan black in tube diluted with japan drier and a dash of varnish. Paint in with No. 2 flat-end red sable brush all these penciled outlines of units.

5. The two end panels are directly edged over the right and left curved thin Windsor spindles. Measure the center of these two small panels and draw in unit No. 8, marking on the linen where the exact top is so it is easily found when you stencil it in over the blacked-in unit No. 8. Make the four cornered compound stenciling by placing unit No. 10 forming a rectangle.

6. Black in with japan black all your penciled outlines and wait until next day to dry thoroughly.

7. With your No. 4 heavy quill striper draw in the ¼ inch broad stripes on back panel as shown, also down the two heavy uprights and around the front of the seat. The fawn or light brown color used for this is made by mixing equal parts of Phillips white, burnt Sienna and raw umber (oil colors). Add enough varnish to make the mixture semi-transparent.

8. With your fine hairline striper, stripe in the black striping as shown. The arrows on top of each of the seven spindles are not necessary, but add interest and were used frequently on the better type of rockers.

9. Next day, when your chair is very dry, varnish the back panel and stencil in the various units in the order you traced them on the panel. Shade the larger leaves with a curved piece of linen.

10. The next day, when dry, wipe off the stenciled area with a damp cloth to remove excess powder. The entire panel is now varnished to protect the stenciling from any mistakes you may make with the black Spencerian scrolls.

The brush strokes are dark green, done with No. 2 red sable brush. The scrolls are put in with a "twirler," a fine long-haired flat-end red sable brush, see page 8.

Wait a day and give your chair two coats of satin rubbed effect varnish two days apart.

You have now a fine old chair, decorated authentically, which will eventually become a cherished heirloom.

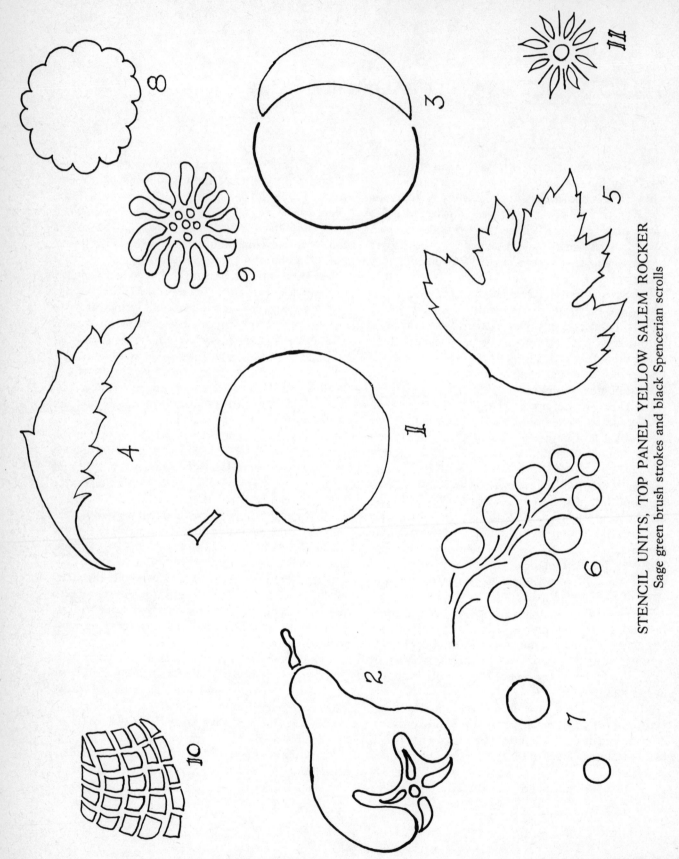

STENCIL UNITS, TOP PANEL YELLOW SALEM ROCKER
Sage green brush strokes and black Spencerian scrolls

82

STENCILED CHEST OF DRAWERS, RESTORED

83

THREE-DRAWER STENCILED CHEST OF DRAWERS

These three- and four-drawer pine bureaus were formerly very plentiful, and practically a drug on the market for years. They have been "picked up" in huge numbers by dealers and finished in natural pine. They lend themselves, however, to stenciled decorations, which show to excellent advantage on the rosewood grain finish. If you have one, try decorating it with the patterns illustrated in this section.

PROCEDURE

1. Sand down bureau. If too rough, remove paint to the wood with paint remover, especially if it has a coat of white enamel.

2. Paint red, Venetian or burnt Sienna in japan, grain, and apply antique stain as outlined in Chapter III. The knobs should always be removed and grained or finished natural mahogany, as desired.

3. Trace on your linen (cut the size of the loose-leaf notebook page) all the units Nos. 1 to 16. Cut these out of the linen. Do not copy dotted guide lines on flower sketch. They indicate shading.

4. If your chest is four drawers, we suggest that you do every other drawer with the same design. Number the drawers inside so you will know where they fit best in the bureau. Measure the center of each drawer with pencil mark, and then varnish with furniture varnish the first and third drawers. In the bureau shown on page 83 we varnished the top and bottom drawers only. If all three were varnished at once the proper tackiness would be lost before we stenciled the top and bottom. Or do one drawer at a time.

Remember, it is helpful to practice a stenciling project on a black-painted cardboard, varnished, before starting on a piece of furniture.

5. Lay your stencil linen with No. 1 unit in the center of the top drawer. Stencil the poppy stamens with silver powder; the edges of the petals to ⅔ down with No. 65 (Both) bright gold. Blend in the balance of the flower with your red gold bronze.

Stencil the poppy on the bottom drawer the same.

Stencil unit No. 2 to the lower right of poppy, the same color combination, and then stencil this unit No. 2 on the bottom drawer in same position.

Wipe stencil unit No. 2 with turpentine dampened cloth. Turn over stencil sheet and stencil the *left-hand* No. 2 unit on each drawer. Next stencil in the four silver daisies, unit No. 3 (above units No. 2).

Stencil in three No. 5 units in silver above the poppy on each of the identical drawers. Next stencil the two left No. 4 units with silver powder blended to deep gold.

Shift stencil to right (do not turn over) and stencil the two right No. 4 units similarly.

With No. 7 leaf unit, shade in three of these units under the poppy on top and bottom drawers, using a straight cut piece of linen for veins. Fade the deep gold-leaf edges quickly and deftly as shown in the photograph.

Next shade unit No. 6, five leaves pointed left, with deep gold No. 65 (Both) for highlight midrib, and statuary bronze from the leaf edges faded to center.

Do the same on the bottom drawer.

Wipe the stencil unit clean, turn over to right side of pattern and stencil five right-pointed leaves, unit No. 6, on top and bottom drawers.

Now all the stenciling is done except the "feathering-out" unit No. 14 which should be placed around the edges in silver powder as shown. The scroll corners unit No. 15 are all put in last over the entire bureau.

6. The center drawer, or, if you have a four-drawer chest, the second and fourth drawers, are now varnished; when it is the right tackiness, stencil in silver or white gold your basket unit No. 8 in the center. No. 11 flower unit is stenciled next, to right of basket, overlapping the basket slightly,

STENCILS FOR THREE-DRAWER CHEST
Do not trace dotted guide lines on flowers

POPPY

ROSE

LEAF

DEEP GOLD LEAF

STAR FLOWER
IN SILVER

15

SCROLL FOR
DRAWERS AND
TOP OF CHEST

14

SILVER

16

IVY LEAF UNIT

13

FEATHERING OUT UNIT

86

STENCIL UNITS 13–16, THREE-DRAWER CHEST

to break the basket's sharp edges. Use silver powder for center of flower and No. 65 (Both) bright gold for outer two-thirds of the petals which are shaded to red bronze at base of flower.

Shift and stencil left-hand No. 11 unit.

Next No. 9 rose is placed in center of basket hanging over the top edge to break the line. Silver and No. 65 (Both) bright gold are blended on this No. 9 unit.

Next No. 10 rose unit is placed to the right, blended to red bronze at base of petals.

The four daisies, unit No. 3, are next put in to the left of No. 9 rose.

No. 12 unit is put in above the center rose.

Stencil No. 12, turn over your sheet and stencil the left No. 12 unit in silver.

The four leaf units No. 6 are then shaded in to fade into the flowers in deep gold or statuary bronze. You can then complete your center decoration with the feathering out units No. 13 and No. 15 in No. 65 (Both) gold by shifting (not turning over the sheet).

7. Now varnish the six corners of the three drawers or the eight corners of your four-drawer chest and the four corners of the top of bureau as well as the deep apron at bottom if there is one. Stencil the three or four right corners with No. 15 scroll unit and the proper corresponding corners on your bureau top. Use either No. 65 (Both) bright gold or No. 108 (Venus) smooth pale gold. Fit the scroll appropriately on the bottom apron and stencil. Clean the stencil unit, turn over and stencil the left-hand corners of the top of bureau.

8. Next varnish the two wide uprights either side of the drawers, and when tacky, stencil unit No. 16 from the top of each to the bottom, repeating carefully the ivy leaf units only. This bronze powder should match the scrolls.

9. When your bronze work is done, the bureau can be striped in a $\frac{1}{4}$ inch gold line connecting all the scrolls on drawers and the top and along the curve of the apron. Use same powder as on scrolls, mixed with this varnish. At two sides of bureau, keep it simple by merely outlining the panels with this wide gold stripe.

10. You now can hairline stripe the drawers, top and apron as well as the side uprights. Use a deep unobtrusive soft yellow, otherwise you will "kill" the whole effect with your bright yellow stripes. It is unnecessary to use the curved hairline at the corners of drawers and apron. This can only be achieved with much practice, but of course adds interest.

11. Next day shellac your bureau with two thin coats of orange shellac 4 hours apart. After 48 hours, rub down with No. 00 steel wool and pumice and oil if you wish. Otherwise give it two coats of satin finish varnish two days apart. After the knobs have been treated to the same finish, your bureau is completed.

ROCKEE WITH HORN-OF-PLENTY DESIGN ON TOP SPLAT
Top design for seat front actual size; also for settee, page 30

88

ROCKER OR SETTEE WITH DETACHABLE RACK
Behind Which the Baby Was Rocked to Sleep While the Mother Sewed or Read

ABOUT 1845

This New Hampshire piece, in excellent condition, is a fine example of the settee on rockers, with mahogany arms like those of the Boston rocker. Manufactured in great quantities at one time, it was almost always in rosewood graining, stenciled, and striped.

STEPS FOR DECORATING

If you have a small settee or a genuine rockee, sand it down, paint red, grain and finish off with the walnut stain, see Chapter III. Scrape the mahogany or cherry arms with a steel scraper and sand smooth with No. 0 sandpaper.

Use same finish for reproduction in white wood.

1. Rub down flat the back panel with No. 00 steel wool and measure its center. This is where the tips of the conventional motif No. 8 meet.

2. Trace on your 8 x 11 sheet of architect's linen the units as they appear, Nos. 1 to 9, shown on page 90.

3. Cut out these units as detailed in Chapter IV, page 21.

4. Trace on architect's linen the conventional pattern on the seat front and the small motif repeated on the front stretcher on pages 88 and 74.

5. Cut these patterns out.

Measure midway on top splat and mark with pencil. Also at one-quarter and three-quarter points.

6. Varnish the back splat and a three-inch wide strip along the front of the seat, and the entire lower front stretcher.

When the varnish is the proper tackiness, place unit No. 1 upon the first pencil mark (quarter way point) showing through the varnish, midway between the curves of the horn-of-plenty. Stencil the two saw-edged rims either side with silver powder.

With No. 65 gold bronze start with the *bob* loaded with bronze at the points of the two horns and fade the gold slightly toward the center.

Stencil solid the two horn tops and cut-out small circles with No. 65 bronze, with the edges, top and bottom of the curved horns brighter than the center (see right-hand horns in photograph, page 88).

Place unit No. 2 between the horns and stencil in with silver powder.

Now with a short piece of curved cut linen, stencil the shaded effects connecting the leaf points of each of the four horns with the saw-edged rim. There are seven of these shadings done with deep gold bronze.

Next, place the peach in each horn and stencil and shade with No. 65 bright gold as shown in photograph. Wipe cut-out peach unit No. 3 with a cloth dipped in turpentine to clean. Turn over peach and stencil it in each horn facing left.

The grapes Nos. 4 and 5 are next stenciled as you have learned to shade individual grapes on page 49. There are six large grapes No. 4 unit in each right and left facing horn.

Continue the bunch of grapes downward with circle No. 5, a smaller grape. There are four of these No. 5 sized grapes in each horn facing left and right.

Next, with unit No. 6, place the leaves as shown in photograph, shading with a straight piece of cut-out linen three leaves, with midrib shaded behind the grapes on all four horns-of-plenty, facing left and right.

No. 7 unit is a feathering-out unit to add interest. Stencil solid with No. 65 bronze on the top of the two right horns, and wipe with a turpentine moistened cloth. Turn over unit and stencil on the top of the two left horns.

The last stencil unit, unnumbered, is the grape tendril which is placed as a feathering-out unit three times repeated behind each group of leaves on two right and left horns. Your center motif of horn-of-plenty or cornucopia in each panel is completed.

PEACH

LEAF

GRAPE

GRAPE

3

6

4

5

FEATHERING OUT

GRAPE TENDRIL

GOES BETWEEN HORNS.
SILVER POWDER

7

2

SEE GUIDE LINES ON 8

9

8

CONVENTIONAL UNIT
CENTER AND ENDS

1

HORN-OF-PLENTY PATTERN, BACK SPLAT ON ROCKEE
Do not copy broken lines. They indicate shading on horns

90

7. The conventional unit No. 8 is now stenciled with point about ½ inch from each end of the rockee or settee by simply reversing (not turning over, because it is uniform). Stencil solid the two No. 8 units in the center of rockee, having the points meet exactly.

No. 9 unit is superimposed on No. 8 in silver powder with the larger oval connecting the two curves of the scroll.

8. Now take cut-out unit at top of page 88 and stencil solid with No. 65 bronze two of these units on the seat front, equidistant from the ends of the seat.

9. On pencil marks at one-quarter and three-quarter points of the bottom stretcher, stencil solid small unit shown on page 74. This completes the stenciling.

10. While the varnish is still tacky, with a quill striper making a line the width of the conventional unit No. 8, stripe the wide gold lines No. 65 bronze by mixing it with a very little varnish and some japan drier to a cream consistency.

Connect up the four units No. 8 at the top and bottom of back panels. The striping in this gold is plainly shown on the back of the seat one inch in front of the twelve back spindles, continuing along the inside of the ends and along the front edge, and is carried along the entire rear of the outside of the seat behind the spindles. The cut corner striping and curves in front add interest, and of course the line is continued along the front of the seat under the two seat stencils.

The turnings are gilded on legs and the baby-retaining rack as shown. All the yellow fine-line striping shows up in the photograph and can be done from this. A help would be to draw in the lines with chalk and straight-edge stick.

Hairline stripes are a deep yellow (chrome yellow medium in japan plus small amount of burnt Sienna, plus a drop of black). This mixture, put in a coffee can cover, should be thinned and mixed thoroughly to a flowing consistency with your japan drier.

The only striping not showing well in the photograph, page 88, is that up and down each of the twelve back spindles connecting two rings around each at the top, and one ring around each at the bottom. This is also done on the two spindles under each arm and the two heavy arm uprights. The striping on the rack shows nicely.

The piece is now complete except for its two finishing coats of shellac applied a day apart, with the final coat rubbed down carefully with 00 steel wool, and wiped with tack cloth. If you prefer not to rub, give it two coats of satin finish varnish two days apart.

You have accomplished an excellent example of early compound stenciling. These rockees, sometimes called "mammy-benches," are fast becoming museum pieces today.

OLD FIVE-FOOT SETTEE, RESTORED, ABOUT 1845
Above is actual size stencil for front seat roll, barely discernible in photo

92

ORIGINAL OLD SETTEE RESTORED

ABOUT 1845

This five-foot settee, while not as old as the rockee pictured on page 88, is an original in size and design, probably done about 1845, but the horn-of-plenty or cornucopia pattern is of earlier origin. We have decorated a vast number of settees which have been made a convenient size by cutting in half the ten-foot-long church settee or bench, adding two arms (Boston rocker arms) and decorating the two-for-one in matched pairs. Illustrated on page 92 is an authentic original, with very interesting and unusual arms.

PROCESS OF RESTORING AND DECORATING

In doing over your old settee, it is not usually necessary to scrape or remove old paint. Sand it down most thoroughly, especially the back panel and the seat. Use No. ½ sandpaper, then No. 00 sandpaper to finish.

1. Your settee could be just as authentic done in old yellow, or coachpainter's dark green (Willey's chrome green light, plus small amount of burnt umber) or it could well be a soft Indian red. See page 9 for mixing the old soft colors. Whatever color you choose, sandpaper it carefully between coats of paint with No. 00 sandpaper. The one illustrated was rosewood grained as detailed in Chapter III. Of course, if you paint your settee *in colors*, even the dark green, the designs where stenciled will have to be *blacked in* as done for pattern No. 1. Do not black in anything for unit No. 12 in center of panel and ends. If painted yellow, stencil these units (11 and 12) in deep gold or statuary bronze and it will show nicely.

2. Cut a piece of architect's linen the size of the book page and trace on it, dull side up, the units 1 to 12. The unit stenciled on the seat roll is on page 92, and on the front stretcher use sketch shown on page 74. Cut out these units very carefully as taken up in Chapter IV. Varnish the back panel with thin furniture varnish and when the right tackiness, proceed as follows.

Divide the long back panel into equal quarters, and mark with pencil. With unit No. 11 in the exact center, stencil solid with No. 65 bronze. Do the same ½ inch from each end. Next, with No. 12, which is half a unit, stencil five of these in a row, spacing nicely either side of center No. 11 and each end of settee.

3. Place unit No. 1 in center of left panel and stencil, and right panel and stencil with No. 65 bronze.

Place unit No. 2 on left panel, left of unit No. 1 and stencil in center with silver powder or No. 308 (Venus) white gold.

The leaf-like points are No. 65, shaded into deep gold, the top star, No. 2, done in silver powder.

Place No. 2 unit in right panel and stencil similarly. Wipe unit No. 2 carefully with turpentine-moistened cloth, turn over and stencil the right-hand horn in each panel.

Next put in the four peaches No. 3 as shown in photograph, shading carefully from No. 65 to deep gold.

No. 4 unit lime is next put in under the peaches with deep gold or statuary bronze if you wish.

Now place the grape bunch No. 5 as shown, graduating the colors: No. 65 at top of grape bunch through deep gold at the smaller grape cut-outs.

Stencil unit No. 6 (two sizes) above these grapes and smaller circles interspersed, shading each grape individually with No. 308 white gold.

Now leaf unit No. 7 is placed at the top of each cornucopia and used to "pull the pattern together."

No. 9 unit is shaded with No. 65 bronze drawn along a curved piece of linen; edges of leaf underneath each cornucopia, right and left, are deep gold shaded carefully towards center.

Unit No. 10 is our very important "feathering-out" unit and goes in No. 308 white gold, repeated twice on groups facing left, cleaned, turned over and repeated twice on groups facing right. This completes the back stenciling.

4. Varnish 3-inch strip along the seat front and varnish the lower stretcher and stencil the two

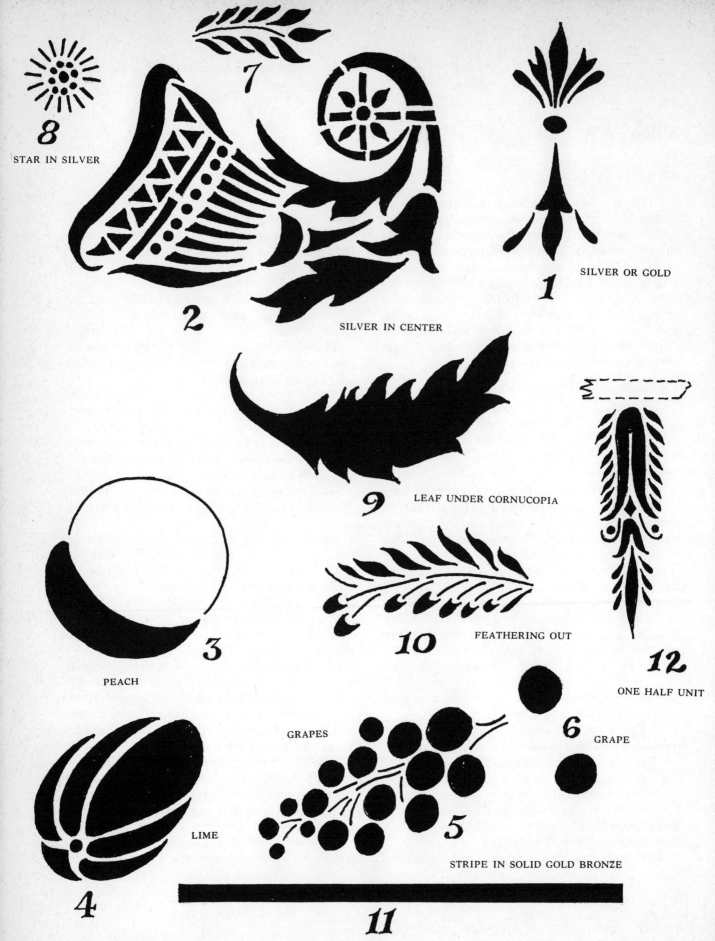

8
STAR IN SILVER

7

2
SILVER IN CENTER

1
SILVER OR GOLD

9 LEAF UNDER CORNUCOPIA

3
PEACH

10 FEATHERING OUT

12
ONE HALF UNIT

GRAPES

6 GRAPE

4
LIME

5

STRIPE IN SOLID GOLD BRONZE

11
SETTEE STENCILS

94

units 4 and 5 (see Hitchcock groups) on the seat (repeated) and front stretcher as shown. This completes all stenciling.

5. Stripe as shown in photograph with only the hairline yellow; a soft mustard yellow if on rose-wood, a brighter yellow if settee is dark green and the same if red. If settee is yellow, stripe in japan black thinned with drier.

Shellac if done in rosewood; if done in colors, use satin varnish as in Chapter VIII.

SIDE BORDER DESIGNS FOR BACK PANELS OF HITCHCOCK CHAIRS
Do not copy broken lines, which indicate edge of stile

CANE-SEATED FIDDLEBACK CHAIR, RESTORED
ABOUT 1845

96

EARLY TYPE FIDDLEBACK CANE-SEATED DINING CHAIR

ABOUT 1845

These chairs have always played second fiddle to the more desirable Hitchcocks, arrowbacks or better type thumbbacks. They now seem to be much in demand. We have stenciled thousands of these with various "fiddle" and "top" designs, and they are rather effective. In the later 1850 types the fiddle was shield shaped (not as desirable) and the legs often square. The chair shown on page 96, one of a set of six, is a good example of an early fiddle or bannister back.

PROCEDURE

1. If you need a new cane seat have it put in after your chair is reglued. Rub down with No. 0 sandpaper carefully and scrape the back panel and fiddle if at all rough.

2. Paint your chair or set with two coats of Venetian red or burnt Sienna, sanding between coats with No. 00 sandpaper. Grain in black and apply the walnut antique varnish. Wait until thoroughly dry and rub flat with 00 steel wool all the areas to be stenciled.

3. On notebook page of architect's linen, trace accurately the one-piece fiddle cut-out pattern, shown full size.

On another sheet of linen trace the top splat corner scroll unit No. 1.

Trace the two side post units No. 14 and the central fruit units, using another sheet of linen. These units are numbered 4 to 13. Now cut out stencils.

4. Varnish the fiddle and two posts with your furniture varnish. When tacky, stencil the fiddle unit using silver powder for the urn and either No. 65 (Both) bright gold or No. 108 (Venus) smooth pale gold for the rest. With a large *bob* stencil powder uniformly, applying gold through the cut-out stencil. Stencil the two posts, No. 14 unit, in matching gold.

5. Varnish the top splat, and stencil in No. 1 scroll unit in right-hand corner. Clean with tur-pentine cloth and turn over the stencil to the other corner with No. 1 unit.

Center the peach unit No. 2 and shade with No. 65 powder as in the photograph. Next shade No. 3 of two-part peach into No. 2 unit.

Shade No. 4 (apple) into unit No. 3 of peach to the right.

Shade in the pear left unit No. 5 as detailed in shading pear, page 52.

Now place No. 6 leaf unit over the pear and shade nicely as shown, with piece of curved cut-out linen along which *bob* is drawn.

Flower unit No. 7 is used twice as in photo, done on silver powder.

No. 8 leaf unit is placed to left of each No. 7.

Next the superimposed strawberry group No. 9 and No. 10 is put on, placing the stems and seeds first in silver. Then lay on the cut-out berries exactly, and shade with red or fire bronze, fading it from the edge of the strawberries toward the center.

The two sized circles 11 and 12 grapes are now placed under the fruit group and shaded in silver individually so that one grape seems to hide behind another.

The final leaf points No. 13 unit can now be placed behind the fruit as shown, fading away. Your stenciling is now completed.

6. Connect the scrolls at top and bottom with a ¼ inch line, using quill striper in the same shade of gold as the scrolls. Put on the gold rings as shown with this gold, mixed in a thick cream consistency.

7. The chair can now be striped with dull yellow hairlines, as the photograph shows.

8. Next day, wipe the stenciled areas with a damp cloth. Shellac two coats of the orange shellac, and when thoroughly dry rub final coat with No. 00 steel wool. If you prefer the rubbed effect varnish, give the chair two coats spaced two days apart.

ONE-PIECE STENCIL FOR FIDDLEBACK CHAIR
Urn in silver powder.   Rest bronze

98

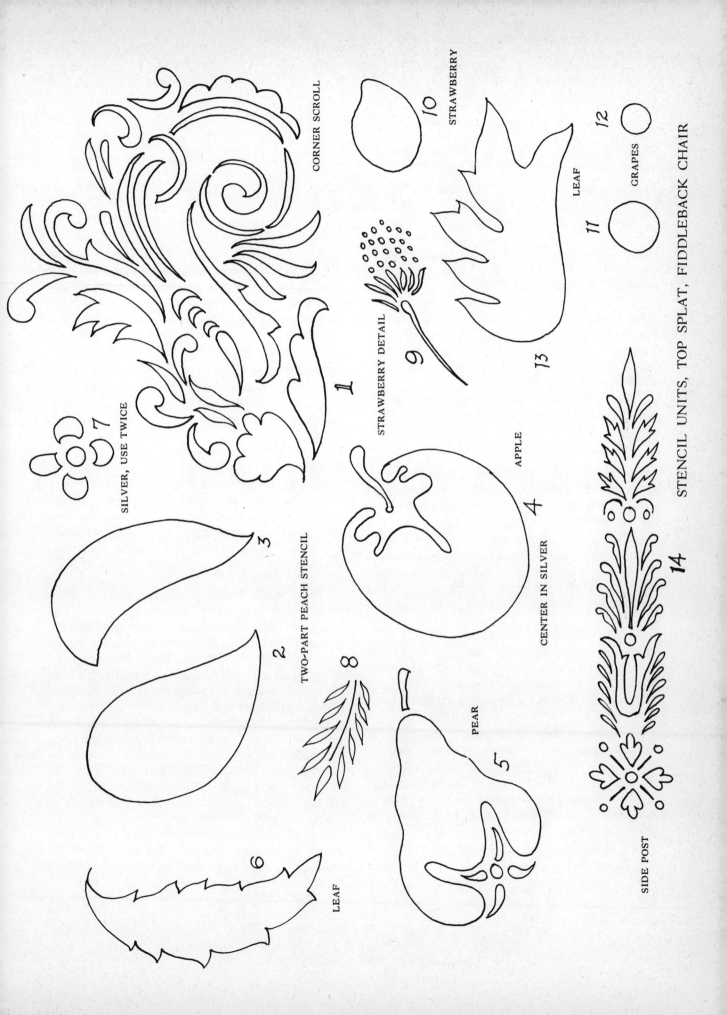

CORNER SCROLL

SILVER, USE TWICE 7

TWO-PART PEACH STENCIL

3

2

LEAF 6

STRAWBERRY DETAIL

1

STRAWBERRY

10

11 LEAF

GRAPES 12

13

8

APPLE

CENTER IN SILVER 4

PEAR

5

SIDE POST

14

STENCIL UNITS, TOP SPLAT, FIDDLEBACK CHAIR

CHILD'S ROCKER

This lovely little child's chair, photographed on page 101, although not signed, is undoubtedly an original done by that master craftsman, William Eaton. It was found in New Hampshire, which seems all the more to verify this, and the painted roses were distinctive with him. Likewise, the delicate, exquisitely cut stenciled bird corners with fine brushwork superimposed on the stencil is unusual. If you have a similar chair or even a child's Boston rocker with wooden or cane seat, this design can be used.

The chair is painted a pale blue-green, striped in white with broad vermilion stripes down the arms.

PROCEDURE

1. Trace on your tracing stencil cloth the corner motif, and the little repeat border that is stenciled around the front edge of the chair. This is intricate cutting, and it would help to consult Chapter IV, page 21.

2. Apply a coat of thinned furniture varnish to the top panel. Stencil the left-hand corner, using deep gold bronze or brushed brass. Do not shade bronze, but apply uniformly to both bird and scrolls.

Next wipe stencil carefully with a clean cloth moistened with turpentine. Turn over the stencil and stencil the right-hand corner. Next stencil the repeat border along the front edge. Use deep gold bronze. Repeat the unit until the entire front is stenciled.

3. The next day, after tracing the freehand painted rose decoration, apply it over a chalked paper to the center of back panel. Next stripe the chair in white, Phillips white plus a dash of varnish.

You will need the following materials to paint this decoration; one small tube of each of the following, in oil:

Phillips on titanium white
Chrome yellow medium

Chrome green light
Alizarin crimson

The left-hand rose is pale yellow with its bud. The right-hand rose is white with upper right-hand bud. The two daisies are dull soft orange. The leaves are two shades of green and the small brush strokes are in old deep yellow and burnt Sienna. The two lower right-hand buds are in soft pink shaded to yellowish green.

PROCEDURE FOR PAINTING

Paint in the entire white rose with Phillips white, also called permalba, to which is added a minute dash of raw umber mixed with a very little clear varnish. Use a No. 3 pointed red sable brush. Paint in the entire left-hand yellow rose with Phillip's white to which has been added a small amount of chrome yellow medium and minute dash of chrome green, all mixed with varnish to semi-translucent consistency. Paint in the colored section of left bud and right white bud, with this mixture. Put in the two right lower buds with white to which a dash of alizarin crimson is added in varnish.

Paint in the daisies' petals with chrome yellow with a dash of alizarin crimson added and tiny amount of white with varnish in single brush strokes. Paint in the centers with chrome yellow softened with a dash of green. Next paint in the stems and leaves in chrome green mixed with your raw Sienna (in japan) to a soft dull sage green. Also now you can put in the small brush strokes with a dull mustard yellow above the white rose and burnt Sienna with a dash of white mixed under the white and yellow roses.

Wait until next day for shading the roses and the leaves and buds. The white rose petals are shaded with clear varnish with a minute bit of white and dash of green and raw Sienna (japan color) added. The center of white rose is pale cream color (white plus raw Sienna). Blend the shading on each rose petal by dipping brush in clear varnish, flattening on newspaper, and with almost dry brush, with quick single strokes, shade from top of petal to base. Shade white bud in same manner.

The yellow rose is shaded by adding more yellow to Phillips white. Each petal is one big sweeping brush stroke with plenty of clear varnish to give it a transparent look. Shade the two lower right buds with more crimson added on lower side of bud.

The leaf shading is with top of brush loaded with green plus more yellow with a dash of crimson to soften. The leaf veinings are done the next day with burnt Sienna with a dash of Phillips white. The shadings and lines shown in the picture on the stenciled bird are done with your finest brush with a mixture of $\frac{1}{2}$ burnt Sienna and $\frac{1}{2}$ raw umber, both oil colors. When your painting is quite dry, after two days, give the chair two coats of satin varnish, one day apart.

ORIGINAL CHILD'S ROCKER

101

FREEHAND PAINTED FLOWER AND LEAVES

DESIGNS FOR CHILD'S ROCKER

102

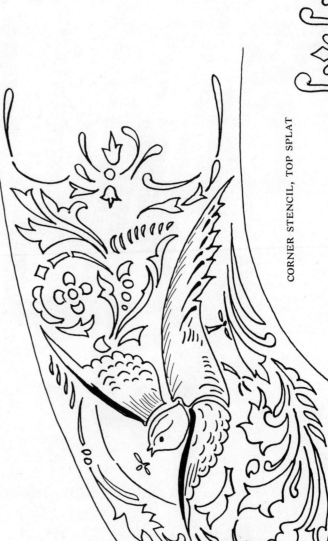

REPEAT AND SEAT BORDER

CORNER STENCIL, TOP SPLAT

OLD COMMODE

This old commode, sometimes called a dry-sink, was stenciled several years ago by the author. While the original commodes were much less elaborate, they were stenciled as a rule on the light grained wood with scrolls in the corners. Sometimes the scrolls were much more elaborate than the one chosen for this example. As stenciling shows up much better on a rosewood grain than on the light grain, we use the dark background. It is a utilitarian piece of furniture, widely used now as a handy bar. These formerly sold for five dollars "in the rough," but now are somewhat higher priced. The top lifts up with a large space inside, and the cupboard inside the door is capacious. The towel racks are usually removed, but were left on in this case. The inside of the top and bottom compartment and drawer is painted in pale green, yellow, or sometimes a soft gray.

PROCEDURE

1. Scrape and sand down thoroughly an old commode, similar to illustration below.

2. Paint it outside with two coats of japan Venetian red or burnt Sienna, a day apart, and sand with No. 0 sandpaper between coats. When thoroughly dry, grain in black and put on the antique walnut varnish stain, see Chapter III. When thoroughly dry, rub down with 00 steel wool to a flat finish.

UNITS FOR OLD COMMODE

SILVER IN CENTER

ALL SILVER

ROSE TERMINAL MOTIF, DOTS IN SILVER

LILY OF VALLEY IN SILVER

SILVER CENTER

SILVER ON DOTS

OUTER HALF PETAL IN BRIGHT GOLD

UNITS FOR OLD COMMODE

6

8

9

10

7

1

5

104

SCROLL CORNER FOR TOP PANEL
AND FOUR CORNERS OF TOP
OF OLD COMMODE

DISH FOR
SIDE PANELS

3. Make three stencil units. On a piece of architect's linen trace the lovely one-piece stencil see page 45 with shaded leaves and meadow pinks, showing the heavy stem #2 separately. On a third piece of linen trace the corner-scroll, page 105 and the small dish, page 105 to be placed at the bottom of the two side panels.

4. Cut out your three traced sheets. Put a thin coat of furniture varnish on entire front of commode and lay commode on its back on the floor, to stencil.

When the varnish is the proper tackiness in the center of the broad panel, stencil flower unit No. 1, using silver powder on the dots, No. 65 bright gold on the outer half of the petals, shading this into your red bronze powder, sometimes called "fire," at the base of the petals. Stencil in the stem in deep gold under the central flower.

Place the large one-unit stencil No. 3 to the left of the central flower. With silver powder stencil the tips of the seven flowers or meadow pinks.

The base of these flowers and centers of the round ones are done with the red bronze powder blended nicely into the silver outer half of petals.

With a piece of curved linen, stencil in the curved midribs of each leaf and the six shadings on the end leaf with No. 65 bright gold bronze by drawing the *bob* along the curved linen. Shade (*bob*) in the edges of each leaf with deep gold, shading to brighter midrib carefully. All the small leaves and stems are done in No. 65 bronze.

The two star flowers are silver.

Lift stencil sheet and stencil the three star flowers over the central flower.

Wipe stencil sheet with a turpentine-moistened cloth. Turn stencil sheet over and stencil the right hand as you did the left.

5. Measure center of the door and place No. 5 unit as the center flower. This has silver center, with outside half of petals done in No. 65 gold shaded to a deeper gold bronze at base of petals.

Stencil No. 6 flower to lower right, using silver powder for center, shaded to deep bronze.

Next stencil No. 7 flower with silver center. The bright gold (No. 65) petal tips are shaded to red bronze at their base.

Next No. 8 flower, above this, is done in silver with highlight at top of flower. No. 8 is repeated lower left.

Place a small silver star, cut in No. 3 unit, upper right. With silver powder, stencil the four right units No. 10, lily-of-the-valley. Wipe stencil unit

and turn over to stencil the left four lilies. The door grouping is now complete except for the leaves with shaded midrib taken from large cut-out No. 3.

6. The two side panels are identical. Stencil the two small dishes centered exactly in bright gold. With the *bob* fading to the edges, dash a little deep gold in the center of each.

Now with part of large unit stencil No. 3 turned over, stencil with same shadings as wide upper panel the five small flowers and three leaves to fill the side panels properly, omitting all the rest of the cut-out. This makes an interesting group growing out of the dish and fits the space nicely.

Fill in each dish with the two leaves as shown. On top of your stenciled five flowers and three leaves, stencil the rose unit No. 9 on each side as a terminal motif, using silver over dots, No. 65 (Both) for petal tips, and red bronze at base of flower, blended well.

For the top of commode (not shown), varnish and stencil a group of flowers and leaves, units Nos. 1–9. Use your artistic sense and you will undoubtedly surprise yourself. All the stenciling left now is the upper corner scrolls, done with No. 104 deep gold lining bronze. There are four of these on the four corners of the top of your commode.

7. With only one cut-out pattern for corner scrolls, it is well to stencil all the left-hand scrolls on your piece, using No. 104 deep gold lining bronze. Then clean the stencil, turn over and do all the right-hand scrolls.

Striping

You now can stripe the ¼ inch bands connecting the scrolls (always with the same bronze as the scrolls), with a No. 3 quill striper. In this case, 104 deep gold bronze (Both) is used. See striping detailed in Chapter VI.

Each section of the sides (not shown) has the ¼ inch stripe ½ inch from the edges and following around its entire outline. The finer dull yellow hairline striping shows up in good detail in this illustration. The loop corners on the door are a trick of the old craftsmen, as well as the quarter circle return corners around the inside of the door panel. The amateur should pencil these in before striping with the hairline striper. Use only the *tip* of the striping brush in drawing a quarter circle. Stripe the top similarly. You can now apply the finishing coats (Chapter VIII), and paint the inside areas any color desired, as suggested previously.

This design, while only one of many used on commodes, is quite effective. Most of the units come originally from Boston rocker top panels.

SHERATON FANCY RESTORED ARM CHAIR AND SIDE CHAIR
Courtesy of Mrs. Foster Reynolds Sheldon, Kingston, R. I.

107

SHERATON FANCY CHAIR

PROCEDURE

1. Prepare your chair with base red coat, black graining and walnut varnish stain for the rosewood effect as detailed on page 14. When thoroughly dry, rub down the walnut varnish stain carefully with No. 00 steel wool to get a flat background for the transferred chalked tracings.

This type of chair is eminently adapted for the curly maple finish as outlined in full detail on page 16.

2. Trace these designs from page 109 on tracing paper: the gold-leaf center back panel decoration No. 1, the gold-leaf front seat design No. 10 and the top stile motif No. 11.

On another piece of tracing paper trace the stenciled cornucopia units Nos. 2 through 7 and the repeat stencil leaf unit No. 9 for the secondary back splat. Trace the No. 8 border cut-out stencil unit which outlines this splat.

3. With chalked back of your tracing paper transfer on back panel the *outline* of the central lyre and scrolls. Be very accurate as this fine scrollwork requires great precision to be effective. Next trace on the *outline* of the front seat conventional unit No. 10 and the top unit No. 11 on the stiles or "thumbbacks."

4. With a fine No. 1 flat-end red sable brush, using your gold size or varnish, fill in unit No. 1 with very carefully executed round finger motion brushwork. With your No. 2 red sable flat or pointed end brush, fill in the chalked seat design and the two units No. 11 on the "thumbs" or "ears" (top of stiles).

5. The gold-leaf ¼-inch stripes on stiles, third small splat, and front bottom stretcher between the legs are sized in with a long-haired No. 3 (squirrel) quill brush dipped in the size or varnish. See details, page 8. The gold-leaf stripe on stretcher is ¾ inch wide. Be sure to "cut" the curved corners of this broad line uniformly if your chair has a wide board stretcher. This gold stretcher panel is copied exactly from an old Sheraton chair

and goes well with the more elaborate seat design. When the almost-dry tackiness is reached, lay on your transfer gold as instructed in detail on page 47.

6. It is well to save time while you are waiting for this sized-applied gold, to gold leaf the rings on the chairs as indicated in the photograph on page 107. A small cotton pad pressed onto the leaf and firming it into the low places in the turnings will help the leaf to fill in the low spots. Wait until at least the next day before cleaning off the excess gold with a soft pad of cotton.

Next day give all gold-leaf areas a thin coat of orange shellac.

Wait four hours and then, after you have cut out the stencil units Nos. 2–9 on the architect's linen, apply a coat of thinned furniture varnish for stenciling these over your two stencil back panels.

7. When the proper tackiness, stencil the horn unit No. 2 so that it fades into the gold leaf. Stencil the five small accenting lines with No. 65 (Both) silver powder onto the gold stenciled horn.

Clean this unit, turn over, and stencil the left horn, which seems to grow out of the gold-leaf base.

Next, unit No. 3 is placed in right and left horns as shown, using No. 65 bronze (Both). No. 4 unit is placed above and below this No. 3 unit and faded into it. The grapes, No. 5 and No. 6, are then placed inside horn as shown. See illustration on page 52 for shading grapes. Then the two-leaf group No. 7 is stenciled behind the grapes and faded sharply, using a curved piece of linen for the veins. The top panel is now stenciled.

Next, on the secondary splat space accurately the No. 9 leaf and tendril unit, and using No. 65 (Both) bright gold, shade the leaves, as shown, with a curved piece of linen, using your very small quill *bob*. The No. 8 surrounding border unit is cut out along the edge of the linen stencil. When cut out this way it is placed on secondary splat, reaching right to ends (near stiles). Be careful with the corners. After stenciling, do 8, 9, 10.

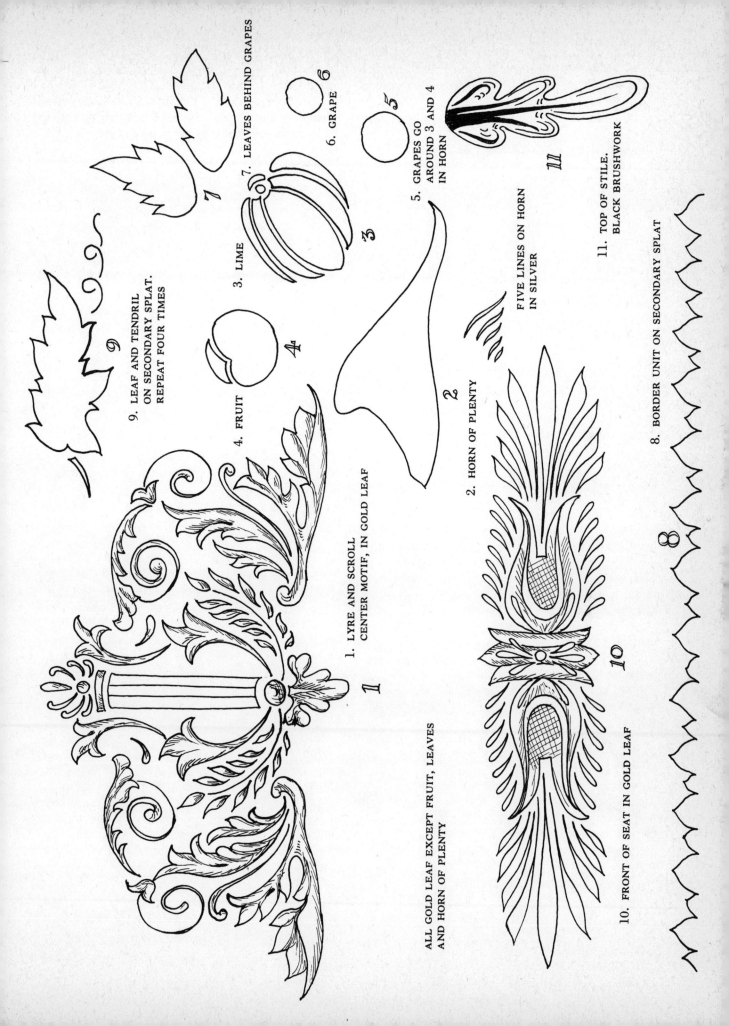

7. LEAVES BEHIND GRAPES

6. GRAPE

3. LIME

5. GRAPES GO
AROUND 3 AND 4
IN HORN

9. LEAF AND TENDRIL
ON SECONDARY SPLAT.
REPEAT FOUR TIMES

4. FRUIT

FIVE LINES ON HORN
IN SILVER

11. TOP OF STILE.
BLACK BRUSHWORK

8. BORDER UNIT ON SECONDARY SPLAT

1. LYRE AND SCROLL
CENTER MOTIF, IN GOLD LEAF

2. HORN OF PLENTY

ALL GOLD LEAF EXCEPT FRUIT, LEAVES
AND HORN OF PLENTY

10. FRONT OF SEAT IN GOLD LEAF

8. Using your fine needle etching tool, etch the large No. 1 unit and the No. 10 front seat unit as precisely shown in the sketches.

The No. 11 thumb unit is fine black *brushwork* on the gold.

9. Now the gold-leaf No. 1 and No. 10 are to be shaded with oil colors burnt Sienna and raw umber mixed. See details on page 108.

10. Next stripe your chair with hairline yellow stripes, as shown, and when thoroughly dry shellac or varnish your chair as taken up in Chapter VIII.

CAPTAIN'S CHAIR
Reproduction with eagle and stars in gold leaf

TAVERN, CAPTAIN'S OR BAR CHAIR, REPRODUCTION

Not long ago it was easy to find this type of tavern chair, as well as several other forms of the popular chair, antique and authentic, at a very low price. This reproduction has become very easy to obtain in white wood and is effective decorated with the gold-leaf eagle detailed on page 113.

PROCEDURE

1. Give chair, made of pine and maple, a thin coat of diluted orange shellac. When dry, sand down carefully and apply a coat of Venetian red or burnt Sienna (ground in japan, thinned with turpentine); see Chapter III, page 14. Next day apply the black grain, and when thoroughly dry, in twenty-four hours, give it a coat of walnut varnish stain, page 15.

2. After rubbing top curved panel, arms and seat with 00 steel wool, trace detailed *outline* of eagle, larger star and top of arm conventional design. With chalked back of eagle and star areas face down on back of panel, trace on eagle and four stars as shown, in outline only. Brush in eagle and star areas with gold size or varnish, and when the proper tackiness, apply transfer gold leaf; see page 47.

3. While waiting for this to dry properly, cut out the scroll from linen and stencil at top of one arm. Clean stencil carefully with turpentine moist cloth, turn over and stencil top of other arm.

4. While waiting for these parts to dry you can put on the gold rings as shown in the photograph, and the wide quill striping in gold powder; see page 40. Along the front of the seat is a ¼ inch wide gold stripe, not shown, as seen around the eagle panel.

5. In about two hours you can stripe hairlines as shown in dull yellow; see page 40.

6. Wait until next day to shade up eagle with burnt Sienna and raw umber mixed to a golden brown color and thinned properly with japan drier liquid with a dash of varnish. This shading is done with No. 2 flat-end round sable brush as shown in gray part of eagle; see page 8. Each star is carefully outlined with this golden brown also. In about two hours this shading will be dry enough to apply the very fine black hairlines on eagle and stars, done with thinned japan black and the finest flat-end or pointed brush you have.

7. After a twenty-four hour period, give entire chair two coats of thinned orange shellac, a day apart, and rub down carefully with 00 steel wool. If you prefer satin varnish, no steel wool rubbing is necessary.

Note: these chairs are very effective done in coachpainter's green (japan chrome green light plus a small amount of burnt umber), and also in dark cardinal red (permanent vermilion, in japan, darkened slightly with burnt umber).

DESIGN FOR CAPTAIN'S CHAIR AND COBBLER'S BENCH

Used on Work Patterns 15 and 16. Actual size eagle in gold leaf. Large stars on chair. Small and large stars on bench. Scroll stenciled top of each chair arm.

113

PINE COBBLER'S BENCH

COBBLER'S BENCH
Reproduction decorated with two eagles in gold leaf and large and small stars

This elaborate copy of an old cobbler's bench is readily obtainable today in white wood, as well as four simpler patterned benches at less cost, and lends itself to the same eagle gold-leaf decoration as the bar or tavern chair, Pattern 15.

PROCEDURE

1. See Work Pattern 15 for finishing white wood furniture.

2. Follow the steps outlined for decorating the captain's chair, Work Pattern 15. There are *two gold-leaf* eagles on this piece, one on the back of seat area and one on the top of drawer section at the end. There are six large stars and four smaller stars on the corners of the top of drawer section. The circle of stars is formed by seven of the smaller stars spaced evenly around the penciled circle on the front section as illustrated.

3. Stripe in gold bronze No. 65 (Both) the outline of the back, seat, all the drawers and the top of the eagle drawer section as well as the two ends of the bench.

4. When the gold striping is sufficiently dry, hairline stripe in yellow all the various surfaces shown, about ½ inch in from the gold stripes. On the legs this hairline is run down in the exact center of every other section of the six-cornered leg.

5. When entirely dry, finish as detailed for the captain's chair.

These cobbler's benches have become very popular as coffee tables, and now as television benches.

114

FRENCH EMPIRE INFLUENCE CHAIR, SOMETIMES CALLED "BALTIMORE HITCHCOCK"
Original Decoration

FRENCH EMPIRE INFLUENCE CHAIR
Sometimes Known as Baltimore Hitchcock

ABOUT 1845

This unusual chair was "picked up" by the author only recently and was acquired solely for the beautiful stenciled and hand-shaded decoration. Fairly well preserved, it could have been done by William Eaton. We had an identical shell decoration on a combback Boston rocker, restored in 1945; also, this same decoration appears on another Boston rocker in Janet Waring's book. The complete pattern of the beautiful top splat appears on page 117, to be traced easily by the progressing amateur. It is one of the most complicated designs in the book to execute, and better not attempted until you have thoroughly mastered the brush stroke technique, both with larger flat-end sable or squirrel-hair quill brushes, and also with the finest show-card brush or "twirler" available.

PROCEDURE

1. This design does not belong exclusively on this type of chair. It would be even more in keeping on a combback Boston rocker. If you have a Boston rocker, prepare it with the rosewood grain finally rubbed down carefully with 00 steel wool as explained on pages 14 and 15.

2. Trace from the drawing entire detailed sketch, noting (a) the shaded brush areas with single hatch lines on the nine shells are done in a real Van Dyke brown, the open (not black) brush marks over and under the shells are fine-lined yellow, the solid black lines are in black (japan); (b) the cross-hatched areas on shells No. 2, No. 3 and No. 9 are cardinal red (your permanent vermilion with a small amount of raw umber added).

3. The central shell is laid-on gold leaf. On a piece of tracing paper, copy the outline of this shell (No. 1). Chalk the back of the tracing. Place this chalked back tracing in the center of your Empire chair or Boston rocker and with a hard pencil go over the shell outline. Fill in the outline with gold size or thinned furniture varnish. When tackiness is almost dry, lay on your transfer gold as detailed on page 47. Wait until the next day to wipe off the excess gold leaf with a soft pad of cotton.

4. While waiting, trace on your architect's linen the *outline* of shells Nos. 2 through 9, and the outline only of leaf No. 10.

Stencil leaf No. 10 on left hand of splat.

No. 10 leaf is stenciled on the right-hand side by turning over the No. 10 cut-out after cleaning the linen unit.

Cut out these 2–10 stencil units as detailed on page 117. The cross-hatched section on shell No. 2, shell No. 3 and shell No. 9 is *not* traced and cut out of the linen, as these three sections are painted in *freehand* with the cardinal red mentioned previously.

Brushed-On Gold Powder Technique

5. You will notice in the photograph of this Empire chair on page 115 that the background for the stenciling of the shells and two leaves is not black but shaded with bronze powder into black behind the shells. This background, exceedingly rare on chairs, is commonly used on the "floor" of Chippendale trays.

The day after you put on the central gold-leaf shell, wipe off the excess gold carefully and varnish the entire back panel. When this is a drier-than-usual tackiness for ordinary stenciling, have ready at hand three shades of bronze on the palette: brushed brass, deep gold No. 3 (Both), and statuary bronze No. 42 (Venus). Make a large *bob* by placing a wad of cotton in a three-inch-square piece of fine woolen cloth or velvet. Dip this pad in your bright gold, and with a circular motion starting at the corners and the bottom of your chair splat rub this brightest of the three bronzes on the tacky varnish. With the pad dipped in the deeper

WORK PATTERN 17, CUT IN HALVES

Joined, it is nineteen inches. Brush strokes to be added. See Baltimore Hitchcock

117

No. 31 gold (Both), place it on the bright gold and gradually work toward the center of the panel.

Next dip the pad into the statuary bronze No. 42 and place this on the deep gold, work back toward the center of panel splat, shading the deep gold carefully into the statuary bronze, which is shaded *sharply* into the black chair background color. All these three bronze shadings should not be over 2 inches deep at the bottom of the panel, 1½ inches deep at the top, and 3 inches at the chair panel rounded corners.

Wait until next day for wiping away the excess powder with a damp cloth.

6. The next step is to stencil in your nine cut-out shell patterns and the two leaves either side of them, as shown in the photograph. Varnish the entire panel and when the right tackiness, shade carefully, starting with the shells Nos. 2 and 3 next to the gold-leaf shell No. 1. They seem to be behind No. 1 shell.

Stencil Nos. 4, 5, 6, 7, 8, and 9, in that order. The leaves are stenciled last, turning over No. 10, after proper cleaning, to stencil for opposite leaf.

7. The next day, when this stenciling is entirely dry, wipe off with damp cloth. To save time and hold the gold powder under a film that will allow wiping off any mistakes, apply a thin coat of orange shellac. This can be rubbed down flat after about three hours. You are then ready for the brush-shaded colorings and the brush strokes on the three-tone bronze shaded background.

8. With the chalked back tracing of the entire design, using a hard, sharp pencil, trace on every detail of the shells, leaves and freehand brush strokes on gold-leaf shell and shaded gold background.

9. Shade in all the single-hatched areas with a golden light Van Dyke brown (equal parts burnt Sienna, raw umber [oil colors] and a dash of japan black with a few drops of varnish added). Use your flat-end No. 2 red sable brush. Paint in the three red areas, cross-hatched, as indicated on the drawings (cardinal red equals permanent vermilion or American vermilion with a slight amount of raw umber), japan colors.

The dotted line on the gold-leaf shell unit No. 1 bounds the top of area to be shaded with the golden Van Dyke brown made much more transparent with clear varnish. Next, with the flat-end red sable brush, or some prefer the No. 13 quill brush pictured on page 8, with black japan (paint fairly thin) stroke in all the solid black brush strokes under the shells and over the leaves traced from design.

You must wait until the next day for the hairline yellow brush strokes on the leaf veinings and *above* the shells as the sketch shows. Use your finest water-color or red sable brush for these.

The finest brushwork *on the shells* is in Phillips white. These do not show up to advantage on the pen and ink sketch, but if you hold a reading glass over the photograph of chair the very fine brushwork on each of the nine shells shows up plainly. This completes the brushwork, which, of course, is the chief unique feature of this chair.

With a fairly large hairline striper, put on the containing black stripe entirely around the panel with japan black, double hairline width.

10. Next day, when entirely dry, give the entire panel a coat of furniture varnish. If your chair is a Boston rocker, stripe and decorate similarly to Work Pattern No. 2 and finish as delineated there. If you have acquired a "Baltimore" Hitchcock with gold-leaf Flaming Torch design, do this in gold leaf and shade up as indicated in the photo, superimposed with oil colors.

You have now accomplished one of the most difficult designs found on the old chairs, and while it may not exactly match the master, William Eaton, you can be justly proud of the achievement.

IMPORTED SWEDISH DINING CHAIR, MADE ENTIRELY OF PINE
ABOUT 1880
Hand-painted, white background.   Leaves in two shades of green.   Flowers in shades of orange.
Courtesy of Blanche Borden Frenning, Little Compton, R. I.

DECORATED SWEDISH DINING CHAIR

This Swedish chair, ancestor of the modern contour-fitting chairs of today, is one of a set brought to this country about seventy-five years ago. It is authentic, perhaps over-decorated by today's standards, but attractive, and strange to say, comfortable. Chests, cupboards, wall shelves and such are commonly imported and sold here, but decorated chairs are rare.

This colorful project is included here because its central pattern (on chair seat front) can be applied to many current-day furnishings in the home. In order to present pattern full size, we show sketch without left end flower. To complete your pattern, simply reverse the right end flower with stalk.

ABOUT THE COLORS

The decorations are applied on a bone white background, painted all in freehand. Finish entire chair with a coat of clear varnish to which is added a small amount of raw Sienna to give semi-antique effect.

COLOR PATTERN

See color chart indicated on drawing, page 121.

Light Yellow Slightly Mustard Color

1. This is used on background of center circle of large central flower, on nearest concentric ring inside dots; next on entire inside area of two side flowers.

Also on the upright leg decoration semi-circle outlining the largest flower and oval buds; see photograph.

Also on the eight semi-circular petals on the central curved top panel (see photograph) which forms the top of chair. This slightly mustard light yellow is also used on two-thirds of the ⅜-inch stripe, bottom and sides of front seat panel as sketched on page 121. This ⅜-inch stripe is the *rare blended stripe*, where the two-thirds width yellow is blended to bright orange one-third of the width with *no perceptible* dividing line, indicated by fine hatched line around sketch.

Bright, Clear Orange Color

2. This color is indicated in sketch on the twelve outer semi-circular petals just outside the dotted circle in the large central flower. Also the dots in each cross-hatching in the very central circle.

On the right and left end flowers the seven petals and the semi-circular outside accent of these flowers are in orange. One-half of the four buds is in orange. This color is brought out well in the seat panel motif as *all* orange as indicated by the single shaded hatch areas.

On the eight-petaled flower on back of curved top panel this orange is used to outline the yellow petals and in dots around the very central black circle.

On the leg upright (see photograph) the orange shades the tiny yellow buds and the extreme outside of the large flower next to the yellow semi-circle. Also the two bracts of the base of this flower on the leg uprights as well as the fine feathery strokes immediately under these are orange in color.

Medium Light Prussian Blue
Secondary Color Effect

3. This is indicated on cross-hatching inside circle of central largest flower, on the eleven pointed petals immediately adjacent. The dots at base of twelve-petal orange center flower are this blue, separating the orange petals from yellow circle immediately inside.

One-half of the four buds (shown black in sketch) are this Prussian blue as well as the bracts at base of two side flowers either side of stem. All other blue appearing on seat panel is the single brush stroke between two outside leaves on right and left flower.

There is no blue on the flower at back of chair's curved top panel, but the leg upright with the semi-circular flower has this light Prussian blue on the main section with the six petals at base put on later with a darker Prussian blue made by adding more tube color.

SWEDISH CHAIR DESIGN FOR SEAT PANEL FRONT
See text for numbered color scheme
To complete pattern, reverse right end flower as left end flower is not shown
Above: Reduced to show both end flowers

121

Light Olive Green

4. This light olive green, the only green used, is not shaded except for the outside one-half area of each leaf; i.e., the *smaller* half of the leaves divided by the heavy black veins. The effect is enhanced by applying a lighter yellowish green with one large brush stroke while the *olive green is still wet*. They will then self-blend.

This olive green appears as follows. Thin circle outside at eleven pointed blue petals, heavy black brush strokes outside of the twelve orange petals and the small brush stroke between each on the extreme outside of the large circular central flower. All stems and fern foliage on bud stems, and bud bracts (eight shown on the base of the four buds). The two heavy curved strokes at base of left and right flower are this green as well as the two fern-like brush strokes either side of the left and right yellow flowers.

On the small sketch for the top panel motif the wide circle inside the eight yellow petals is olive green as well as stems and the four fern-like right and left motifs. On the leg upright design, the heavy black strokes at base of blue flower are green as well as all stems and the fern motif above the blue flower. The fern motif above the two largest leaves here is the bright orange.

Black Accents — Japan Black Thinned with Drier

5. All heavy leaf veins, small brush strokes around leaf edges and the very fine dotted motifs growing out of the left and right yellow flowers are black.

The oval and crescent and the oval at base of each of these flowers are black as well as the heavy black outline shown at the extreme top of each of these flowers.

On the leg upright, see photo, blue flower, these same parts are black, as well as the darker Prussian blue petals outlining appearing in black.

On the top panel, see photo, the central flower has black only on small centermost circle and the three brush strokes between each of the eight yellow petals.

This yellow, orange and two shades of Prussian blue color combination is most effective, but if you wish, other color combinations can be worked out in reds, pinks, etc., to complement your room's color scheme.

122

PENNSYLVANIA BALLOON CHAIR
Painted dark olive green, with one-piece stencil on fiddleback slat

PENNSYLVANIA FOLK ART DECORATION

While the New England artisans and their work are the principal subject of this volume devoted especially to their chairs, it is very necessary that something be included on the so-called Pennsylvania ("German") or Dutch decorations. Their art inspired directly by the old country influence is more colorful and quaint than that of the more subdued New England. There are many exciting books on this period of early decorating detailing their universal love and various interpretations of the Tree of Life patterns, the unicorn, the flattened heart design, the tulip above all, as well as the conventionalized rose and pomegranate. All of these flower motifs were usually placed in various stylized urns or bases. These units as well as the "hex" designs on barns everywhere in Pennsylvania were in gorgeous colors and their chairs were usually in brighter colors than the New Englanders used. The chests and chairs were usually brown, "Dutch" blue, a dark olive green, see the balloon chair, page 123, a light blue-green and even a faded salmon pink.

Beautifully painted dower chests with peasant designs, adapted from German and Swiss inspiration, were brought to their height of perfection by the two Seltzers, Christian Seltzer of Jonestown, Penn., 1747–1831 and his son John Seltzer. In their workshop, fortunately, they trained other artisans or pupils — Johann Rank, John Peter Rank and Peter Rank of Columbia County, Penn. Christian Seltzer was painting and dating these chests from 1771 to 1796.

The earliest of these Pennsylvania tulip, vine and animal designs are found on birth certificates in original vivid colors, now faded to soft beauty, and are known as "fraktur." The schoolmasters who were the originators of this charming art were masters with pen and ink, drawing the outlines of vines, flowers and leaves with the pen and filling in the motifs with the colors. There have been so many marvelous volumes written about this Pennsylvania art that we are showing only one so-called balloon chair with its stenciling detailed.

Pennsylvania Stenciling

While the stenciling in Lancaster, Lebanon, Berks and Bucks counties was not as intricate nor unit-shaded as much as that of New England it was far more colorful. The stencil sheets were usually cut in one unit design with mostly fruit for the central motif. This fruit was shaded in colors; red, green, blue and yellow oil paints were laid over the gold stenciling, which was a fast method of getting the effect of hand painting. Pennsylvania balloon chair illustrated, page 123.

Two Pennsylvania Dutch Chairs

(1) A SO-CALLED BALLOON CHAIR, OR MODIFIED "FIDDLEBACK"

(2) A "LANCASTER CHAIR"

This original balloon chair was painted "stiegel" or dark olive green. It is decorated with the late period one-piece fiddle stencil cut-out, shaded in the central part of flower fiddleback unit, and fruit top panel unit with oil colors, superimposed on the gold stenciling.

PROCEDURE

1. Paint your similar chair, which can be a reproduction in white wood, with two coats of chrome green light to which is added a little less than half the amount of burnt umber (japan color), the mixture to be thinned with turpentine to smooth brushing consistency.

2. Trace the four units, see pages 125, 126, directly from the book on your architect's linen, using four *separate* pieces the proper size. Cut out these tracings as detailed on page 21.

3. Varnish first the bannister or fiddleback panel, and when the proper tackiness, after measuring the exact center of panel, place the pattern centered properly and with a large *bob*, stencil in the entire cut-out unit with No. 31 (Both) gold

PATTERN FOR FIDDLE SPLAT

125

Corner Top
Splat

Center Top
Splat

SEPARATE STENCILS FOR PENNSYLVANIA BALLOON CHAIR

Seat Front

126

bronze. *No* shading is required, except central oval motif.

4. Varnish the front seat section and the right side and middle of the top panel, and when the right tackiness stencil these units uniformly with the same No. 31 gold bronze powder.

5. Varnish the left corner of the top panel. Clean the corner unit with a turpentine-moist cloth (both sides), wipe dry with a clean cloth, turn the corner unit over and stencil the left top corner of panel.

6. While waiting for the stencil areas to dry, put on the gold rings as shown in the photograph on page 123.

7. Mix a deep brown (more golden than Van Dyke) by adding equal parts of burnt Sienna and raw umber to a small amount of japan black. Add a dash of chrome yellow medium, if the brown is not golden enough. With a medium sized quill striper (see No. 12 on page 8), put in the curved striping ¼ inch wide on the seat as shown in the photograph. This stripe is also on the front of the front legs between the gold rings. In the wide Pennsylvania striping in various colors, unlike the New England, which was semi-transparent, it is always an opaque stripe.

8. The fairly bright yellow stripes, as shown in the photograph, are not hairline but fairly broad, and can be made with about fifty hairs in your made-up striping brush. Stripe in the yellow as shown.

9. Next day wipe the stenciled areas with a damp cloth to remove excess gold and when dry give the entire chair a coat of varnish or thin orange shellac.

10. When this is *entirely* dry, shade in the peach, the strawberries and the large central flower on the fiddle with tube oil color alizarin crimson to which is added a small amount of clear varnish. The grapes on the top panel and the smaller flowers on the fiddle are shaded with Prussian blue (oil color) to which a small amount of varnish is added.

11. In about two hours, when this is almost dry, the details are put in with the yellow color used for the striping with your small camel's-hair brush.

12. Next day give your chair a coat of satin varnish or two thin coats of orange shellac. If the shellac is used, rub down in twenty-four hours with No. 00 steel wool.

Pennsylvania "Lancaster" Chair

PATTERN AND INSTRUCTIONS BY WESLEY NORTHEIMER, DOWNINGTOWN, PENNSYLVANIA

A great deal of the decorating done by the Pennsylvania amateur painters, notably the Mennonites, was off balance. They knew little or nothing about perspective or light on shadows. Sometimes they would use a rough pattern, but as a rule they just painted, or, as one we knew expressed it, in heavy accent, "Just giff me a brush and some paint and I'll make a wonderful nice fancy out of my head." Out of his head is right, as illustrated in accompanying design. We do not refer to the skilled decorator, of course, who very carefully laid out his pattern so that it balanced.

PROCEDURE

To ¼ pint of deep chrome green add ¼ teaspoon of Prussian blue. Thin to creamy consistency with turpentine. Add about 3 drops of japan drier. Give the chair two coats of this mixture, allowing plenty of time for each coat to dry hard. When last coat is hard, sand with No. 0 sandpaper. Clean thoroughly by dusting, and then give it a good coat of spar varnish. When this is dry, rub dull and clean with No. 00000 wet-on-dry sandpaper and water. When clean it is ready to decorate.

Copy decorative designs from page 129. Rub a piece of white chalk on back of pattern. You are now ready to trace the pattern on the chair. For decorating, use a No. 3 sable scroll brush; for striping, use a No. 5 camel's-hair striper for the broad line, and we use a dagger striper for the fine line; but if you are just starting, perhaps you had better use a No. 1 camel's-hair or skip the fine line. Better leave it out than have a sketchy line. Thin your tube paints with turpentine. First paint the background of the "wings" on the top slat yellow ochre. When this is dry transfer your patterns as directed.

Color Guide

A.	Alizarin crimson	C.R.	Cadmium red
B.	Black	T.R.	Tuscan red
L.G.	Light chrome green	W.	White
P.	Pink	C.Y.	Cadmium yellow
O.	Orange	L.Y.	Light chrome yellow
		D.Y.	Deep chrome yellow

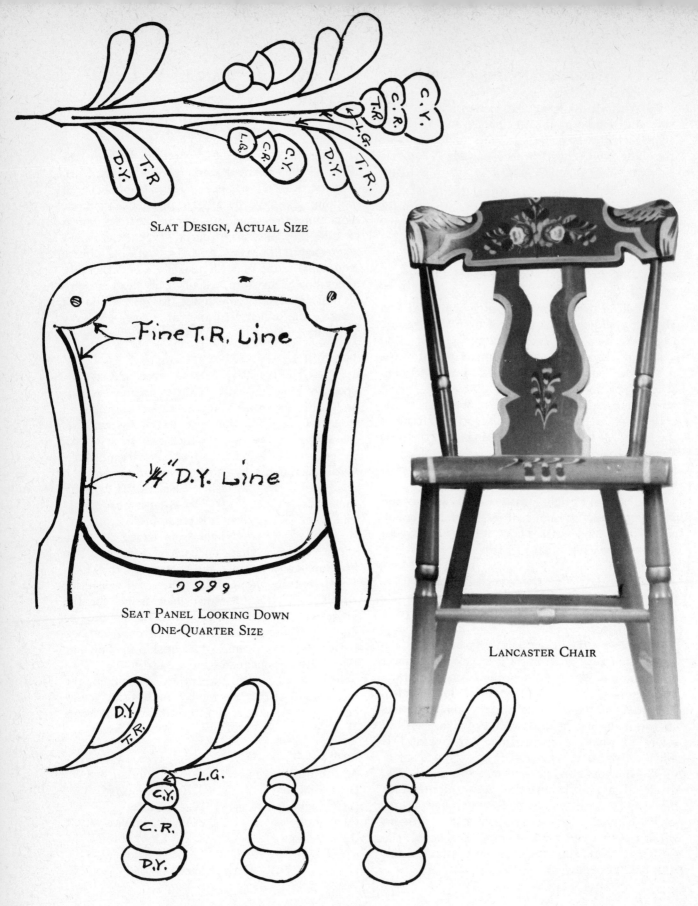

SLAT DESIGN, ACTUAL SIZE

Fine T. R. Line

¼" D.Y. Line

SEAT PANEL LOOKING DOWN
ONE-QUARTER SIZE

LANCASTER CHAIR

SEAT ROLL DESIGN, ACTUAL SIZE

DESIGN FOR LANCASTER CHAIR

128

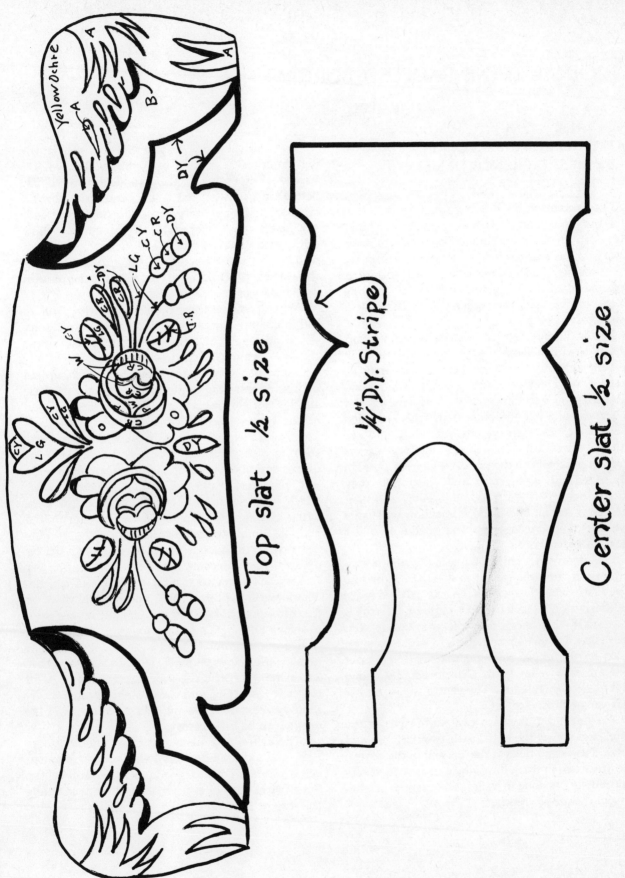

Yellow Ochre

Top slat ½ size

¼" D.Y. Stripe

Center slat ½ size

DESIGN FOR LANCASTER CHAIR

129

ORIGINAL HAND-PAINTED BUREAU

ABOUT 1840

PATTERN AND INSTRUCTIONS
BY MRS. FLORENCE HAMLIN,
LEXINGTON, MASSACHUSETTS

The decoration on this bureau is so lovely in color and painted so freely and spontaneously that it is worth spending the time to learn how to paint flowers in this manner. The technique will prove very useful in doing all kinds of decorated furniture. Once mastered, it will give a method of painting which may be done very quickly with completely satisfactory results.

The background on the original bureau is a soft light tan, with elaborate scrolling and striping in semi-transparent white, but other colors may be used. Old yellow, medium greenish-blue or old white are good, and the stripes may be done in color to harmonize. All the roses, with the exception of one which is bright yellow, are white and red with red rosebuds. The daisies and bud sprays are different colors on each drawer, varying through blue, dark red, soft yellow and violet, but they all have accents of dark red and yellow or white. The leaves are all one shade of medium soft green with dark blue-green veins and shadows in flat color. All stems are vermilion.

The illustration on frontispiece shows the two center roses from the second drawer; the right rose is yellow. The two daisies on the left here are medium dark blue (cobalt) with white brush strokes on the left half drawn in while the blue is wet. The center daisy is alizarin crimson with vermilion petals on the upper side and the small sprays of buds are dull yellow with alizarin accents and a bright yellow highlight. The center is raw umber with yellow brush strokes.

The bottom drawer has two white roses in the center and one at the right, with two dark red and yellow daisies and buds at the left and in the center. The other two drawers have white roses with daisies and bud sprays done in violet, with yellow accents on some and red on others.

To paint these flowers you will need the following materials: a pointed quill shader size No. 10, varnish, turpentine. Also oils in these colors: permalba, cadmium red light (vermilion), alizarin crimson, cadmium yellow medium (in Devoe cad. yel. pale), raw umber, oxide of chromium, yellow ochre and Prussian blue. Use clear varnish as a medium. Use lithopone rubbed into the back of the tracing paper and a stylus to trace the pattern on the drawer.

When painting these flowers, keep the paint to a thin creamy consistency, because these roses are semi-transparent and the background color shows through, helping to shade the flower.

To paint the white rose first, take cadmium red light and locate the center of the cup and the base and lower right-hand side with a few large strokes of alizarin to accent further the base of the cup. The rest of the rose is painted with *white only*, starting with the small petals on the outside edge of the cup and blending them delicately into the wet vermilion center. The two principal petals which form the outside body of the cup are done with a circular brush stroke which is swung around and filled in almost in one motion.

Next do the outside petals in one or two strokes apiece; when you come to the red just put in a few fine white strokes to suggest the edges of a petal. The alizarin center is then added with three or four strokes and two white dots are put in the center of the circular petals as shown.

Do not attempt to work over this flower. The petals must be put on *freely*, with decision and then left alone. Experiment with consistency of paint to get it just right, and then go ahead quickly. It should take only a few minutes to complete if the result is to be satisfactory.

The yellow rose (second drawer) middle group, right rose, is painted precisely in the same manner, using cadmium yellow medium instead of white. Start with vermilion and alizarin and complete the rose with yellow.

Vermilion

Solid dark - Alizarin

Rose on left - white
" " Right - yellow

Daisy - Alizarin & Vermilion

HAND-PAINTED ORIGINAL BUREAU FLOWER UNIT, SECOND DRAWER

131

SCROLL CORNERS, HAND-PAINTED BUREAU

132

The dark red daisies are painted first with single brush strokes of alizarin. The top is then painted with vermilion strokes on top of the wet alizarin and a few fine vermilion strokes to suggest the edges of the lower petals. The center is raw umber to which a little Prussian blue is added. Finish with clear yellow brush strokes around and on the center while wet.

The yellow daisies are painted the same way with yellow ochre dirtied a bit with umber. Add a few strokes on the shadow side with alizarin which will blend with the ochre and highlight with strokes of cadmium yellow light. The center on this daisy is alizarin to which a little umber is added; the small dots around the center are turquoise blue.

The blue daisies are done with medium dark blue (Prussian, umber and white). One half is then painted with very light blue strokes over the wet foundation, and a few fine white lines accent the edges of the petals. The centers are dark alizarin with yellow strokes around the edge.

On the third drawer, which has two white roses in the center and a reversed rose on the left side, the two daisies on the right are painted with the lower half in soft violet (Prussian, alizarin and white) and the upper half yellow ochre with clear light yellow brush strokes over the yellow ochre and a few yellow accenting lines on the violet side. The centers are vermilion with yellow strokes around the edges. Buds are flat violet with a yellow light on one side.

The center daisy is violet with vermilion brush strokes on the bottom half. The center is raw umber with yellow strokes around it. The bud sprays are violet with a yellow light and dot underneath. The spray at the bottom right is violet with a vermilion accent.

The two violet daisies on the right side of the third drawer have white strokes on the petals instead of yellow. The daisy to the left of the reversed rose in the center has a yellow ochre undercoat, with two alizarin strokes on the right, violet petals pulled over at the base and clear yellow ones at the top.

All rosebuds are done with a foundation of flat vermilion accented with one alizarin stroke and a twist of white for the highlight.

The three left-hand reversed roses have vermilion at the base. Start the white petals at the outside edge rather small, and work larger toward the base where they will blend with the vermilion foundation.

For the green leaves mix oxide of chromium with raw umber and a little white and paint all leaves smooth and flat with thin paint. For the veins and shadows use a fairly dark blue-green (Prussian, umber, yellow and white). Use this green very thin with fine brush strokes. All stems are straight vermilion.

Top of bureau has corner scroll work in semi-transparent white, similar to the drawers. See page 132 for full size pattern of scroll corners applied to drawers and bureau top. Use your imagination freely, and decorate the rest of the bureau top to your taste.

EAGLE DESIGN, ONE-PIECE STENCIL

While the shaded or etched gold-leaf eagle is not too uncommonly seen on chairs and chests, the cut-out stenciled eagle is rarely found. Taken from the top of an old wooden document box grained in rosewood finish. It could well be used to ornament wooden boxes or chests

134

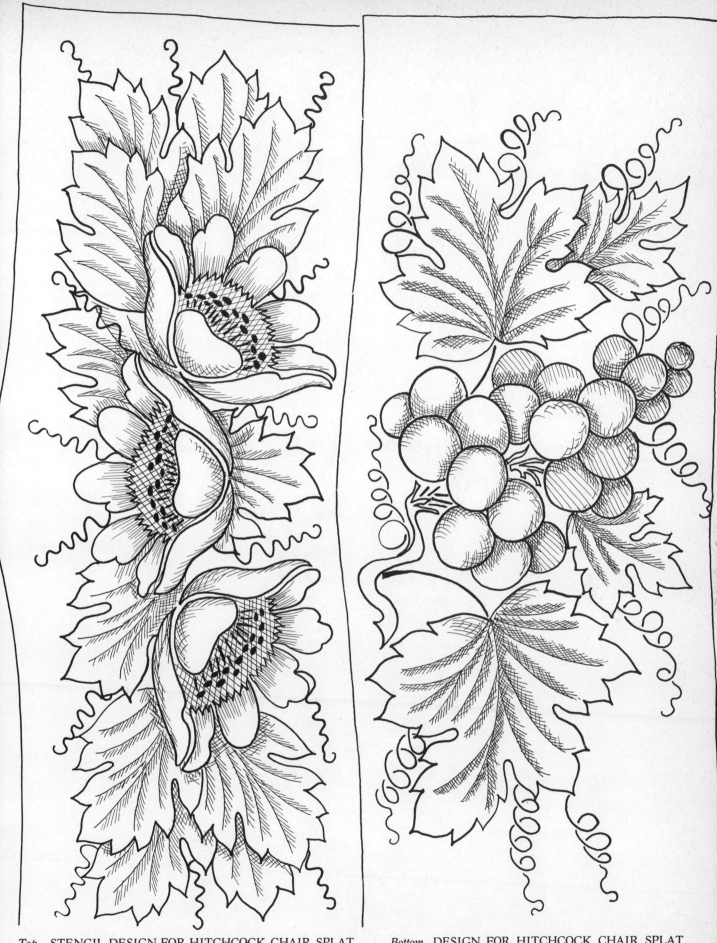

Top. STENCIL DESIGN FOR HITCHCOCK CHAIR SPLAT
Hatched lines indicate bronze shading with curved linen
Reduced from original size of twelve inches

Bottom. DESIGN FOR HITCHCOCK CHAIR SPLAT
Use different shades of gold powder on grapes and leaves
Reduced from original size of eleven inches

STENCIL DESIGNS FOR STILES (UPRIGHTS) ON HITCHCOCK CHAIRS
No. 1 may go on three-part Hitchcock settee, see page 30

PINEAPPLE DESIGN FOR BOSTON ROCKER PANEL
Original fifteen inches wide. See next page for separate stencil units

STENCIL DESIGN FOR BOSTON ROCKER (ARMLESS SEWING) SPLAT
Original seventeen inches wide. Corners stenciled. Bird and fountain brush work

137

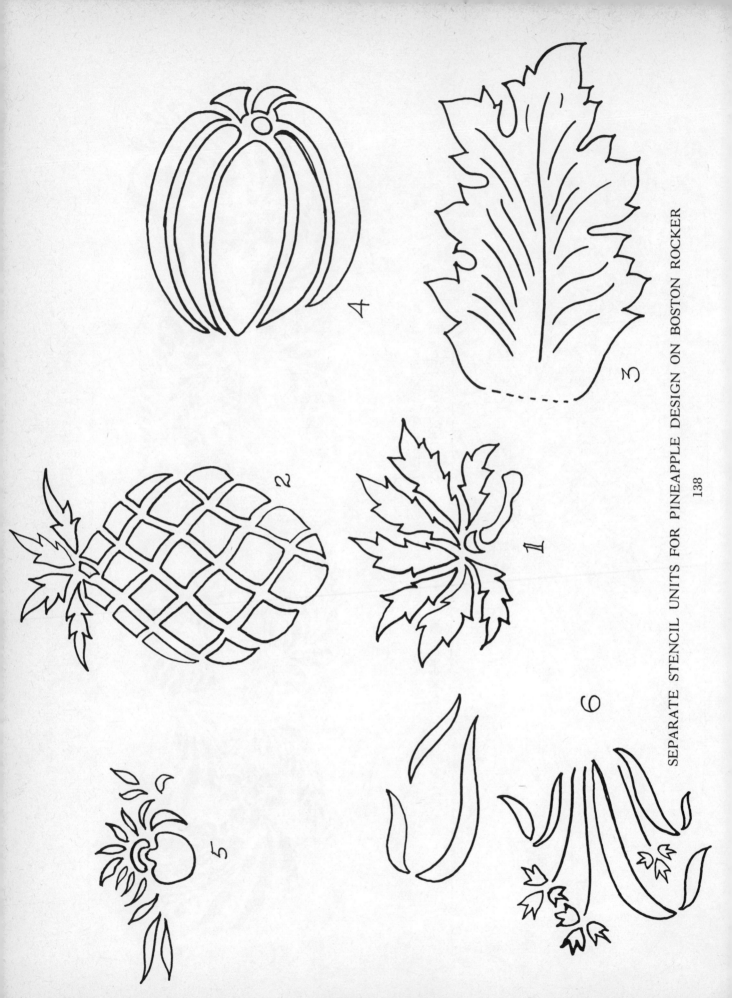

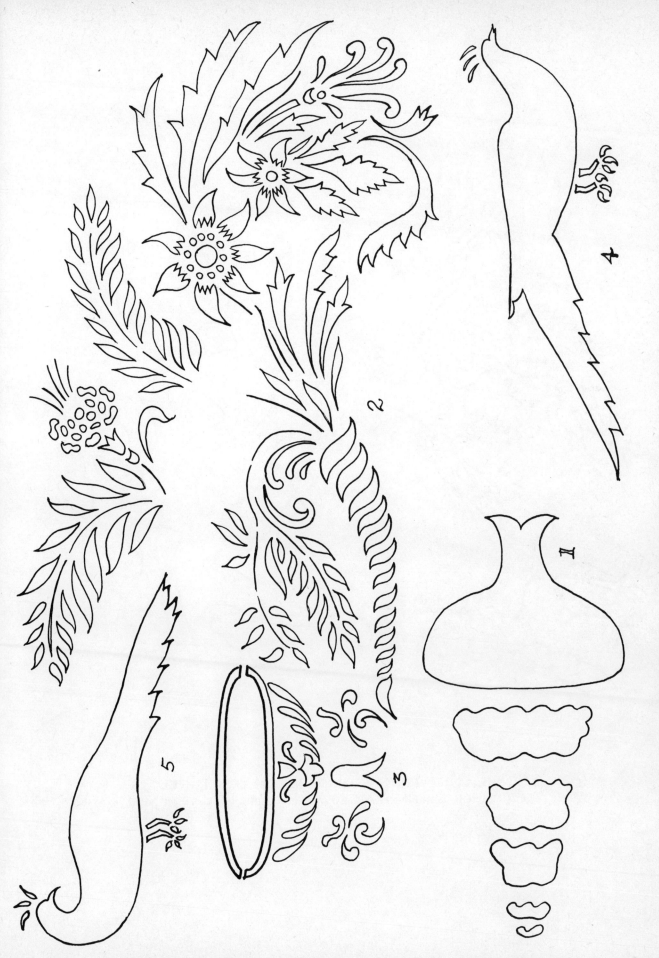

SEPARATE STENCIL UNITS FOR FOUNTAIN AND BIRD DESIGN
BOSTON ROCKER PANEL ON PAGE 137

STENCIL UNITS FOR TWO-ROSE HITCHCOCK PANEL
See page 28. Stencil as numbered. Turn over No. 2 and left petal on No. 1

140

STENCIL DESIGN FOR BOSTON ROCKER CORNER

Attributed to William Eaton. First do No. 1, etc.

STENCIL DESIGN FOR HITCHCOCK CHAIR SPLAT.
CONVENTIONALIZED CORNUCOPIA MOTIF

Reduced from actual size of twelve and one-half inches. See page 143 for separate units

DESIGN FOR A BOSTON ROCKER PANEL

Original (eleven inches wide) was shaded with oil colors over gold stenciled powders. An easy motif

142

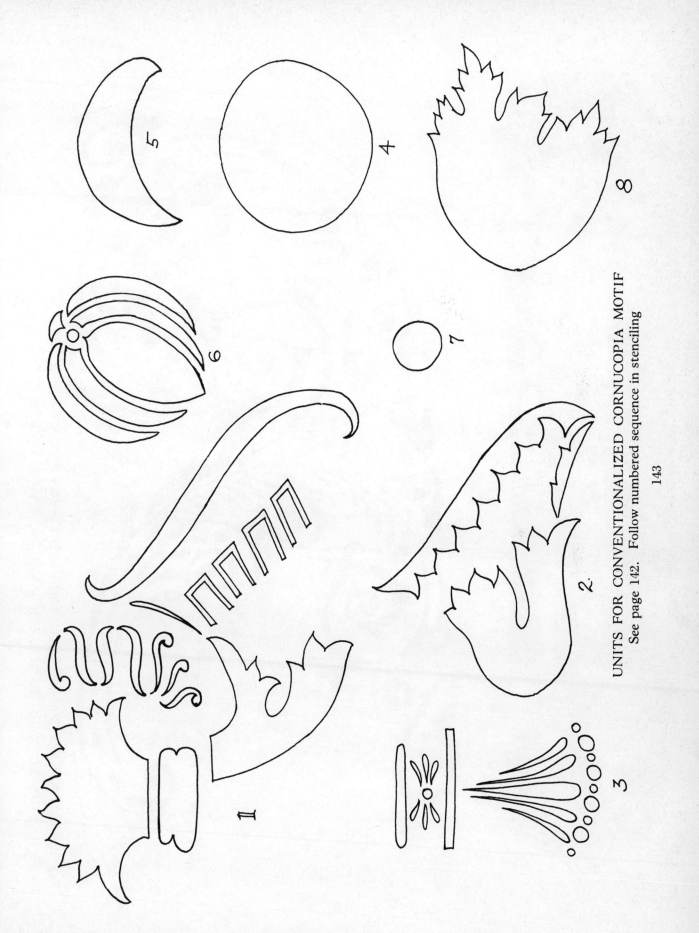

UNITS FOR CONVENTIONALIZED CORNUCOPIA MOTIF
See page 142.   Follow numbered sequence in stenciling

143

Top. BOSTON ROCKER PANEL WITH RARE MULTI-UNIT STENCIL

Bottom. BOSTON ROCKER CORNER, ONE-PIECE, NO-SHADE STENCIL

INDEX